'HAWKEYE'

'Racing drivers are, inevitably, strongly individual personalities. If they were the sort of people who did what they were told from 9 to 5 they wouldn't be racing drivers – or they wouldn't be any good.
They are the highest exponents of one of the most difficult and dangerous arts in the world, and it's no good expecting them to behave like members of the school second eleven.'

John Wyer

'Hawkeye'

*The rapid and outrageous
life of the Australian
racing driver*
Paul Hawkins

IVAN McLEOD

MRP PUBLISHING LTD
PO Box 1318, Croydon CR9 5YP, England

First published 2003

British Library Cataloguing in Publication Data

A catalogue record for this book is available from the British Library

ISBN 1-899870-67-9

Typesetting and origination by Jack Andrews Design, Westerham, Kent

Printed and bound in Great Britain by MPG Books Ltd, Bodmin, Cornwall

Contents

Preface

by Vic Elford

Some while ago, Ivan asked me if I would like to write the Foreword to his book on the life of Paul Hawkins. I agreed, but now, having read the manuscript, I wonder what I am going to say because everyone quoted in the book seems to have already said it!

Like Paul, my first motorcycle was a 125cc James two-stroke with a three-speed gearbox and a hand shift! But any similarity between the two of us probably stopped there, other than the fact that we both came from similar backgrounds...oh yes, and we both won the Targa Florio in a Porsche!

Neither of us started with money, and neither of us started with family support. The only thing we both had to start with was a passion and a will to succeed. And nobody succeeded like Paul. He was unflappable and unstoppable in everything he did.

As you read the pages of this book you will learn language and expressions that will surprise you and perhaps in some cases even shock you. Unlike many of today's 'stars', Paul never spoke unless he had something to say, and he never uttered a word that he didn't mean. Colin Chapman was another dedicated man who was also single-minded in his quest for perfection and eloquent in his expressions. The only time I ever saw Colin at a total loss for words was after a Touring car race at Silverstone. Paul, in the first appearance of the then 'new look' Ford Lotus Cortina, and I in a Porsche 911, had a race-long duel, and when it was over we returned to our side-by-side paddock parking areas. When Colin asked him of his impressions of the car, Paul was able to swear about it for two minutes solid without ever using the same word twice!

Although he had success with them, Paul and Porsche never quite hit it off, but since they were at totally opposite ends of the personality spectrum this was hardly surprising. One day we were testing at the Nürburgring with the new 907, which in effect was virtually a 910 with the bigger, heavier and more powerful 2.2-litre eight-cylinder engine in the back instead of the lightweight six-cylinder 2-litre. After one lap Paul came back and told Helmuth Bott, who was in charge of race engineering, that with the extra weight the rear of the car 'was going up and down like a whore's drawers at a pile driver's picnic'! Fortunately, Helmuth was such a straight, innocent man that he hadn't a clue what Paul was talking about. You will read that such an outlandish expression had other uses, too, and they could only come from Paul.

As you read on, you will come to appreciate how lucky I was. Despite our long friendship, I never had occasion to ride as a passenger with Paul at the wheel on the road! The exception was the RAC Rally that we did together in John Sprinzel's Sprite. But that was OK because as designated night driver and daytime navigator, I was effectively the car manager, so when Paul was driving he did what I told him!

Despite his apparently rough exterior, he could ooze charm and persuasion. Jo Siffert and I had spent a long time trying to get Porsche to allow us to make adjustments to the cars when we were testing, but the Porsche attitude was always: 'The car has been designed for this track. It is perfect.' Only when Paul added his voice to ours did Porsche finally allow us to start making our own adjustments during testing and practice.

From the moment one set eyes on him and saw that infectious grin, everyone was drawn to him, men and women alike. The story you will read about his concern for Christabel Carlisle was typical of his concern for others, no matter who they were.

On that terrible day at Oulton Park, racing lost a great driver and character... and the world lost a great man.

Introduction

Paul Hawkins. Savour the name, and dream on the past. It is a time and place of memories. Of challenges. And Champions.

Somehow, we instinctively know when we have met a very special person. Even if only for a short while. Quite how they influence us is difficult to define, but they leave us feeling richer for the event, and even though it may be years later, we continue to recognize and value their touch in our lives. In preparing his story it soon became clear that Paul Hawkins was one of these people.

Though it is decades since he was of this world, the strength of his friendships and memories of his determination and outrageous humour are a tribute to his special nature. So many times I was told how he was a great friend, a real mate, and heard stories of his generous help. He was a happy person, one who brought light, life and fun into places regardless of social propriety, and sometimes perhaps because of it.

He could drink like a fish, swear like a trooper, and next morning go out to win the race. Women were naturally drawn by his rugged facade and devil-may-care attitude, whilst his view of them was once famously observed when he said they should be kept in either the kitchen or the bedroom (and there is strong evidence to suggest that he preferred the latter, even if he did enjoy his ravioli).

He hated pomposity, disliked authority, poked two fingers at the law, derided religion, and wasn't afraid to speak his mind in the most basic of terminology. He was a one-off, and a very special person in a world where so often it is money that otherwise does the talking.

Whilst he had no family fortune to rely upon, no business connections to explore, no educational qualifications to exploit, and no resources other than his own natural initiative and raw talent, it was his sheer bloody determination that made the difference. It was apparent in the way he left home, in the clarity and single-mindedness of his ambition, and it expressed itself in the way he drove a car.

His racing peers came from wide ranging backgrounds. A few had family support, others a financial stability he could only dream of, and some – like Paul – made it the hard way; rising from urban obscurity to claim applause at the zenith of their chosen sport. Whatever their background, the list of his co-driving peers reads like a motorsport roll of honour, of whom those remaining are unanimous in their desire that his achievements should be recognized.

Jacky Ickx; David Hobbs; Jackie Epstein; Vic Elford; John Sprinzel; Rolf Stommelen; Frank Gardner; Timo Makinen; Warwick Banks; Mark Donohue; John Rhodes, and many more too numerous to list, took easily to his laconic style, dollops of fun, and occasional larrikin-like behaviour. (**Larrikin** – *Adj.* Aust. Vernacular – A cynical yet healthy disrespect of authority – usually youthful.)

His tenacity and determination on the track were legendary. His name synonymous with fast, hard and often dramatic driving, be it in a Sprite, a big Healey or a Lola, while his trademark power-drift overtaking thrilled spectators wherever he raced. Within one whirlwind, madcap year he was factory driver for Ferrari, Porsche and Ford; the three key contestants of the 1967 Sports Car Championship. He would win the Targa Florio in record-breaking time with Porsche, then for good measure hand the Paris 1000 Kilometres to Ford alongside team-mate Jacky Ickx.

In the same crazy year, in his own unmistakable bright red car, he would begin the process of becoming the world's most successful Ford GT40 privateer, winning the UK *Autosport*

Championship. Whilst the South African Springbok series would be his just a year later in the fabulous CanAm Ferrari P4, he would then help Ford clinch the '68 Championship in the famous blue-and-orange cars as a member of the Gulf-sponsored John Wyer team. By 1969, Paul Hawkins Racing Ltd was a fully fledged team, campaigning not only a spanking new Lola T70 Mk 3b, but also competing in Formula 5000 as the development arm of Lola Cars GB; and the future beckoned. It's an impressive record for a kid from the backblocks of suburban Downunder.

Off the track he was charming. A genuine character, able to hold his pint in true egalitarian tradition alongside either mechanic or industry mogul. His blunt phraseology and use of the Great Australian Adjective added further to a colourful language, in which it is said he could expound for 10 minutes without repetition. He could be blisteringly frank, hilariously outrageous, determinedly dedicated to a task, the most loyal of friends, and was without doubt one of the greatest sports car drivers Australia, or the world, has ever produced. Those who knew this laughing, ruggedly handsome, boyish rogue thought him indestructible. Until Oulton Park.

He was always self-assured and calm behind the wheel. When his road car scored 360-degree spins or suicidally rode the red lights at 100mph in the teeming London traffic, he would continue talking to his terrified passengers as though absolutely nothing had happened.

It was surprising, then, when he was seen hopping agitatedly from foot to foot as he waited impatiently for the slicks to be refitted in the middle of the Tourist Trophy race. Maybe he needed a decent placing to help finance the Lamborghini he had just ordered. Perhaps he was thinking of the racing team he proposed for next year. Whatever. The weather had done its worst, and the track was drying fast. He needed to be out there.

Regaining the circuit, he again set his 450bhp Lola off after the elusive lead he had held for the first eight laps. Chasing down the pack and making up places, he was lying in seventh place on lap 75 as he swung into Island Bend in his usual full slide. The Lola slipped wide, searching for grip as it ran onto the grass verge, ploughing into an empty marshals' post. Catapulting back, it smashed into a tree and flipped over before falling back to erupt into a dreaded fuel and magnesium-fed conflagration that snaked across the track. It was an accident of the worst kind. The race was stopped; and the indestructible one was no more.

Whether a tyre failed, or the end of a rear radius-rod pulled out – as believed by his mechanic Richie Bray – remain conjecture even today. What is certain is that on that memorable day the world lost a great character, and a great many lost a great friend.

Today, more than 30 years after his fatal crash, there remain so many of those friends who, on hearing the name 'Hawkeye', break into broad grins, chuckle and gladly share their memories, for he clearly influenced their lives in that indefinable yet very special way that leaves them – and us – the richer.

Acknowledgements

I never did get to meet him, but Paul Hawkins has had quite an influence on my life. I first watched him drive at Surfers Paradise, where my passion for endurance sports cars ignited, and later, as I followed his career with growing admiration, I was shocked and saddened to hear of his demise.

A lifetime later I went searching for his story, only to discover that none existed, and once again Paul entered my life as I worked to correct this undeserved omission. One way or another, he has been part of my experience for the best part of a decade, and in researching his story it has been a pleasure to meet so many others whom he so clearly influenced in his inimitable style.

To them I owe a considerable debt of gratitude, for without their generous and willing help this book would never have seen the light of day. Such was the impact of Paul's strength and personality that everyone who knew him encouraged me in my efforts, each giving freely of their time and valued memories. Many who had only ever heard of his exploits were just as enthusiastic, and all so totally behind the venture that developing Paul's story was always a pleasure.

For putting up with my constant hammering on the keyboard, incessant thirst for both knowledge and drinks, and my one-track mind over the past four years, I must thank Sue, my partner and wife. Her support and belief has been invaluable. Others behind the scenes include my photojournalist friend of 20 years Ron Spillman, who painstakingly proof-read my scrabblings, photographer Mike Pritchard for his invaluable skills, Paul Gates for his brilliant cartoons, and Graham Heath for use of his remarkable archive.

Thanks are also due to Vic Elford for his support in providing the Foreword, and who, like so many others, was prepared to make the time available to share his memories of Paul. In this latter respect I should particularly like to thank Richie Bray, Jackie Epstein, John Hawkins, David Hobbs, Jacky Ickx, Peter Jackson, John Pledger and John Sprinzel.

For their contributions and generous help, I would also like to express my sincere thanks to the following: Jannie van Aswegen (South African Guild of Motoring Journalists), Richard Attwood, David Baker, Robert Barker, Mike Brown, Christabel Carlisle, Tom Coulthard, Bruce Dowling, Paddy Driver, Ray English, John Etheridge, Frank Gardner, Barry Green, John Green, Owen Holmes, John Horsman, Graham Howard, Richard Hudson-Evans, John Love, George Makin, David McKay, John Miles, Bernard Mooney, Bill Morris, Doug Nye, Bob Olthoff, Nancy Phillips, David Piper, Roy Pounder, Brian Redman, Howard E Robinson, Graham Robson, Cedric Selzer, Chris Skeaping, Nick Skeaping, John Stillard, Steele Therkleson, Jeff Uren, Ian Walker and John Winter. It is their stories as much as Paul's that bring with them the smell of Castrol R.

My thanks also to *Autosport* magazine for the use of their material, the BARC for their most courteous assistance, Terrific Stuff Ltd for the John Wyer quote, and Pooks Motor Books for the generous use of their material.

Ivan McLeod
May 2003

Chapter One

Son of a preacher man

To William (Bill) and Vivien Hawkins: A Son – Robert Paul. Born Melbourne, October 12th, 1937.

Tasmania 1955

Being a minister of the apostolic church, with a very distinct aversion to bad language, must have had its disadvantages for Bill Hawkins – as could parenthood – and this was definitely one of those occasions. He had returned home to his church in Burnie, Tasmania, from an interstate meeting only to find that his family car, a '53 FJ Holden ('Australia's own car' as they said in the advertising) was distinctly the worse for wear, its rear arches much lower to the ground, giving it a rather racy appearance. Without doubt, both rear springs were broken, and it wasn't too hard to guess which of his three offspring was the culprit.

Paul was two years older than his brother John, and a further two more years separated him from their sister Ruth. Neither of the youngsters was likely to have been responsible for the state of the car, so what had happened?

Having never driven a car alone before, Paul had decided in his father's absence that the opportunity to have a go at an unofficial Penguin hill-climb was simply too good to miss. Unfortunately, miss he did – and the car's state of disrepair was down solely to over-enthusiasm. In defence, he offered a muted:

'Well, at least the car is still drivable'. Thankfully we may never know the reverend's reply.

With driving ambitions suitably pruned for the moment, Paul continued his electrical apprenticeship at the nearby paper mill, where his growing interest in both bikes and cars soon turned to reality in the shape of an old James two-stroke with its rigid rear end. His brother John recalls: 'It didn't last long. It was much of a wreck anyway. His next bike was a BSA Golden Flash 650; laying chin-down on the fuel tank along the Ridgley Way straight, his best speed was 118mph – but it was never fast enough for Paul.'

Seeds of intent now grew ever stronger, and with no way of getting his hands on the family car again, he became absolutely convinced that to have any chance of competing in motorsports he would have to head for Melbourne. John continues: 'Of course, Paul knew that Dad wouldn't have a bar of him leaving the apprenticeship and heading for Melbourne without a job, so while Dad was away Paul packed his bags to catch the passenger ferry *Taroona* the next morning, and without giving notice to his employers, or saying farewell to anyone, and after handing the Golden Flash over to me to sell, he was on his way.'

Such determination and independence had been hard won since childhood, and four years after his mother's death in 1944 the family had moved from Melbourne to the sunny and sub-tropical environment of Brisbane, where their high-diving champion and carpenter father was about to take up his posting as a minister. It was a good move for the young family, though times were difficult.

'This was Dad's first appointment as a minister of religion', recalls John. 'In addition to doing his ministerial work and looking after us three kids, he also built the first apostolic church in Brisbane (it's still standing today), and did nearly all the carpentering work on his own. Paul was only seven when Mum died, so you can imagine, with a one-parent family whose Dad was seldom home evenings and weekends, we were left to our own devices to a large extent.

'Paul was always the ringleader in the neighbourhood gangs. We would always find some form of mischief, or invent it, and if it wasn't turning house mains light switches off (sometimes pinching the fuses from beneath the house), it was placing a box with string attached in the middle of the road at night to test the drivers' reflexes. They were mostly the normal harmless boys' tricks.

'Up to the end of our school days, of course, we were made to go to church/Sunday school regularly (three times on Sunday), but even then there was nothing angelic about our behaviour, even on Sundays! If word got back to Dad about any misbehaviour, then our punishment was to be made to go to church on Tuesday and Thursday nights. Somehow, though, Paul would always wriggle out of this punishment, with me ending up doing the penance. There was a saying back then that the sons of ministers and police officers were always the worst behaved in the street.

'In looking back we always maintained that our days in Brisbane were the best, with such a great outdoor climate and the free and easy life it offered. During the school holidays Dad would borrow some camping gear and a tent, and we would head off for a week, camping at places like Caloundra, Maroochydore and Tewantin.'

It was here that Paul's love of watersports, and his solid 5 foot 11-inch rugby-esque physique would quickly develop, and as the Hawkins family grew, so too did Paul's interest in cars, as John recalls:

'Dad always did his own mechanical repairs and servicing at home on his cars and Paul would help. Dad would say that Paul as a boy of 12 could undertake minor mechanicals, adjust brakes, service the Austin A40, and understood how a car engine worked.

'It was during his time at Industrial High School, until '54, that Paul worked after school and over holidays at Barnes Auto, which gave him his first real association with cars – bowser-boy, grease monkey, etc. He was an excellent scholar, but really had no interest in school. I can't ever remember him doing homework. He was good at sports and could have been successful at most of them, but working weekends at Barnes Auto he really gave sport away for the chance to work with cars.'

Little wonder then that by the time the family had moved to their father's second ministry in Burnie, the seeds of driving ambition, allied with his strongly independent nature, were beginning to create relationship difficulties.

'Philosophically we learned the basic life issues of ethics and morality', continues John, 'doing good to others, compassion and, of course, discipline from our father, but by the time Paul left Tassie at age 18 his ambitions and directions in life were already completely opposed to Dad's ideals and beliefs – including the demon drink and smoking. I think it would be fair to say that Paul was of such strong character, determined to succeed at any cost, that nothing would stand in his way. He was his own person.'

So it was that the *Taroona*, as it crossed the Bass Straight heading for Melbourne, carried a young Paul Hawkins, his ambition now fired by determination. His youthful experience had led him not only to reject his father's beliefs, but to view religion itself as a repulsion that would now influence the rest of his life. His natural teenage rebelliousness would mean that the usual societal expectations of a steady career and all that goes with it could take a proverbial running jump, and like a great many other Aussies of that time he had developed a healthy disrespect of authority, the expression of which was firmly rooted in the exploits of an earlier character by the name of Ned Kelly.

In dealing with officialdom he would brook no argument, and his methodology might well have been based on the famous bushrangers' stand. 'My way or the highway' would later describe his forthright attitude, while it seems safe to assume that some of his parental influences overflowed into a dislike of false finery and affected self esteem, for in later life on numerous occasions he would deliberately set out to puncture the balloon of pomposity. Now, with a twinkle in his eye, a huge sense of fun, and sheer brute strength of character, he was off to see where that driving ambition would take him in the metropolis that was Melbourne.

It led to Percy Makin's Heidleberg garage, where for a living he was soon greasing cars and filling petrol tanks at the Simca dealership, whilst settling into accommodation in the neighbouring northern suburb of Macleod. Finding his aptitude and application appreciated by the owner's sons, Percy and George, they were soon blasting about the backblocks of Melbourne.

His first car was George's triple-carb FX Holden, but as the Makin brothers were able to show him the way in their MG TCs, he soon saw the light and changed it for another TC. George vividly remembers that time, saying of Paul: 'He was a typical larrikin Australian. Back in the Fifties we were pretty straight-laced. The women were straight-laced and there were no 'F' words or anything like that – except for Paul. He had plenty of them flying around to our embarrassment at times.' And it was typical of him that he couldn't have given a 'flying f**k'.

It seems that authority figures, or institutions such as the Law, would never hold any sway with Paul, his larrikin behaviour being epitomized by an occasion that George has good reason to remember: 'We got caught by the cops for speeding', he says, but unfortunately he called Paul as a witness for his defence, which was not a wise thing to do. 'He stood up in court and said: "Your honour, if anyone ought to be charged with dangerous driving I think it should be the police." Of course, there was total uproar in the courtroom . . .'

The local magistrate, unhappy to be charged with the additional task of bringing his court to order, soon slapped a driving ban on George. It was a typical example of Paul's well-honed ability to drop others into the mire, a skill he had perfected in his earlier days when brother John usually ended up doing the penance. Meanwhile, even though he was a partial instigator of the speeding event, Paul continued driving at his usual 100mph through the streets of the city; a behaviour that would eventually get him the sack from Makin's. The old man could no longer abide the works-liveried utility being thrown around in a manner that reflected so badly on the dealership's good name, and Paul was out on his ear.

By now, as was often the case with teenagers, he had met up with a number of like-minded mates, including Owen Holmes, and within a few short months the TC wasn't up to the job either. Paul determined that it should be transformed – into an Austin-Healey. Owen well remembers that wet Sunday night when he and Paul went to pick up Jim McEwan's Healey in the pissing pickaxes of a Melbourne downpour. 'I had a BN1 in those days and gave Paul a lift up to Croydon to take delivery of the car. It was a red BN2, which was basically modified to 100M specification, including a four-speed 'box and a louvred bonnet. We headed back with Paul leading and he just took off, disappearing into the mist.'

The gang were soon practising their low flying around the streets of Melbourne, and could often to be found in Owen's shed working on their machines. 'Paul was very knowledgeable about cars', continues Owen, 'he could make anything work, and with that car the police couldn't catch him, and they chased him every time he drove it!'

Surprisingly – if indirectly – it would be that bastion of authority, the Australian Government, which would offer Paul his real break into motor racing when he was called up for National Service. From all reports, the Army life suited 3/775837 R.P. Hawkins, and after completing his basic training at Pukapunyal Camp, he was posted to instructing recruits in the delicate art of motor transport driving at an Armoured Corps C.M.F. Unit, where he soon made Sergeant.

Here, amid stories of racing armoured cars, he made friends with a young Italian he'd met at 'Puka', who introduced him to his brother – who happened to own an Austin-Healey 100S. One of just four in the country, it was reputedly the Earls Court show car, and a rare beast in any part of the world at that time. A quick trip around the block at his usual speed, with owner Terry Valmorbida sat in the passenger seat, soon had him offered a racing drive. 'He seemed most impressed', Paul reportedly said, 'but then he was probably frightened to death.'

Drives at various local hill-climbs were soon followed by his first real track experience at Phillip Island where, leading the race, he spun out on the last lap, though he quickly recovered to retain a class first. It was an encouraging start. Later in the year saw him again drive Terry's car in the Melbourne Grand Prix meeting at Albert Park, where the cream of Australia's racing drivers had gathered, including such notables as Stan Jones (father of Alan), Bib Stillwell, Alan Mildren, Len Lukey, and a certain Mr S. Moss.

Event Nine was the Sports Car Scratch Race. Terry's car had been entered in the name of his family's business – F. Agostino & Co Pty Ltd – and Paul was well amused that he would be driving a car sponsored by a grocery store. Forty years on little record remains of Paul's race, but fifth for a beginner in such august company was pretty good; even if the car had spent most of the previous night being straightened out after he had redesigned it in a practice shunt.

The year 1959 brought a new job at John Roxborough's Mobil garage, on the corner of Coventry Street and Kingsway, just a mile or so from the racing circuit at Albert Park. Roxborough would later become the Australian importer of Lotus cars, but at the time he campaigned a 1.5-litre Cooper *monoposto*.

At the garage 'Hawks', as he was then known to friends, was kept busy with the string of Healeys crammed onto the forecourt, but it was his exploits that workmate John Stillard best remembers: 'We used to have competitions in the driveway. There were bowsers down the bottom and some at the top and we would throw buckets of water all over the drive and have figure-of-eight races round the bowsers, while John Roxborough (a future C.A.M.S. senior official) used to sit up in a corner of the shower room and be Clerk of the Course; if we touched a kerb we would lose points.'

One Saturday morning Paul turned up with an enormous 21-foot length of two-inch copper pipe and proceeded to replace the exhaust system on his Healey. He then started her up without bothering to shorten the pipe. John Stillard continues: 'It was a magic noise, absolutely magic. It sounded just like a 250F Maserati. We used to do a lot of tuning of Austin-Healeys and other things and used to drive them down (to Albert Park) and back again. Paul just couldn't help himself.

'He took off, and we could hear him going all round Albert Park lakes as he changed up through the gears. The pipe was wired up a bit, but there must have been 12 or 15 foot of it hanging out the back! Anyway, he came past the garage waving his arm out of the car in a gesture to lift something up and pointing – and there was a police car (the omnipresent Mk 2 Zephyr) pretty close behind. We worked out he wanted the roll door up, and so he did a few more laps of the various blocks around the place then came skidding sideways onto the

'Get prepared for a pitstop, I'm coming in next lap!'

driveway, up onto the hoist and we put the door down. But the exhaust pipe was still sticking outside the door about 10 feet so we couldn't get it fully down. We held our breath as the police car came past looking for him, but that's the last we ever heard of it.' Of course, it wasn't the last time he'd be chased by the boys in blue.

Some time later he took his boss' Cooper for a 'fettle down at the Park', neglecting to mention to its owner that it would not be on the trailer. This of course would have been perfectly acceptable to Paul, as the Park was 'just down the road a bit'. However, the Law took a somewhat different view of driving an untaxed, uninsured, full-throttled open-wheel racing car in amongst the Holdens and A40s of Melbourne traffic. The next John Stillard saw of the rapid Formula Two car, it was belting past the garage at full tilt being gamely harassed by a bog-standard police dog van. It was an unfair match, and neither the dog nor its handler saw hide nor hair of him again.

'I remember we played a trick on him once', says John. 'He

Easy win on the streets of Melbourne. The police dog van was no match for an F2 Cooper with Paul aboard.

was tuning a 100M Healey after hours as a bit of a freebie and we hooked an electric spark plug tester up to the spokes of this Healey. He was working on the distributor and kept complaining about a faulty condenser. He just couldn't understand where the shock was coming from. It went on for a fair while, but he ended up catching me. He took me out on the driveway late at night and covered all my private parts in bloody axle grease. He was a pretty wild bloke like that.'

He was also still determined to get into motor racing. He had already worked out that in order to progress in his chosen sport he would need to head elsewhere, though the impetus was not entirely forthcoming until he got chatting with fellow enthusiast Bruce Dowling. Bruce had recently returned from two years' service with the Department of Native Affairs, in Papua New Guinea, and had got to know Paul at Makin's, where his car was serviced.

Bruce had mixed it in his TR3 with others of the gang, including Billy Hughes, who had access to some aviation fuel. As he puts it: 'You are going back to 1959, and the fuel wasn't too good, so Billy Hughes would rock up at the appropriate point in time with a can full of this Avgas. We used to put this stuff into the TR3 and all the rest, and drag 'em all off. God only knows what we did to the engines.'

They traipsed around various events together, including the Geelong sprints. 'We'd been to a boozer somewhere, and we were going home and got lost up some bloody dirt roads in this bloody rabbit paddock out the back of Geelong! Next moment I see lights flashing around the bloody trees. I thought God, who's that, a bloody farmer in a tractor? Next moment 'Hawks' comes round this bloody corner sideways and roars up the bloody road, right up the arse of me TR! Y'know, me neck's a bit sore, and I got out of the car and said: "What the bloody hell did you do that for?" He said: "Jeezes, why didn't ya leave yer bloody lights on?" So I replied: "They were, yer silly bastard, but you were sideways, so how the f**k would you know?"

Needless to say, Bruce wasn't quite ready yet to settle into the

24

family's textile business and decided it was time to see some more of the world, saying to Paul, Owen, and other mates: 'I'm going to England. Sell up, sell the car, get rid of the sheila.' He continues: 'At that stage most of us were running into financial crises in so much as we all reckoned we were underpaid; we were running expensive cars; all smoking most probably; drinking like fishes; and trying to run a sheila – and of course you run out of money. The easiest way to solve this was to go.'

Bruce investigated the options, discovering that they could get to Europe via Panama on one of the frequently returning migrant ships for just £140, and he promptly laid plans to buy a Mercedes, which would enable him to turn a tidy profit on his return to Australia. Paul, however, was not taken with Bruce's idea of getting off in Lisbon for a bit of summer, nor had he the cash to buy a Merc. He and Owen Holmes opted for London while other events soon persuaded Paul to confirm his plans. An 80mph accident on Toorak Rd meant there was a preliminary court hearing which would very likely lead to serious consequences. Within a fortnight Paul had joined Bruce and Owen on board the Sitmar liner *Fairsea* and on the 20th of December 1959 he was off for England with his worldly belongings: a toolbox, the grand sum of £28 and a crash helmet.

The trip across was great fun, and Bruce hints that a keg of rum Paul purchased in Curacao provided some memorable entertainment, but it is his recollections of Paul's character that shine through. 'We always laughed that Paul could swear for five minutes without drawing breath or repeating himself (usually about Pommies), but he had an obsession with speed. Not only was it an obsession, but he could turn off everything else to the point of mind fixation. It was remarkable.' He insists though that Paul wasn't one to take advantage of others. 'I never thought he was trying to achieve by riding over the next bloke. It was a passion; an ambition to achieve, and the joy of youth. The desire to do it, along with sheer devotion and enthusiasm.'

Having dropped Bruce off in Lisbon, they reached a sodden

Southampton on the 4th of February 1960 – an England with a reputation for nine months of winter and three months of bad weather. Bruce would look around Europe before joining up with them later in London. In the meantime, Owen Holmes, Paul and another mate set off to see what this new bit of the world had to offer and they rented a Standard 10 in which to see 'the neighbouring villages of Cornwall and Scotland' (the UK seems very small to most Aussies).

Owen remembers parking in one of the narrow lanes leading through a small Cornish village, aided by Paul's simple expedient of bending the 'No Parking' sign down so that it was hidden by the car. Unfortunately, on leaving, the redesigned street furniture did little for the car's bodywork, and the little Standard was returned to London with quite a few more dents and scrapes than originality dictated, along with four rather bald tyres. Paul Hawkins had arrived.

Chapter Two

Up, up and away...

Sunday, April 30, 1960. Aintree GP circuit.

Two weeks previously Paddy Gaston had pranged his Sprite at Brands Hatch in his desperate attempt to beat the flying Van Niekerk's GSM Delta. His car had a reputation as being a very hot machine, and by now the remaining Sprite camp were beginning to despair that either Van Niekerk would not be beaten, or it would take something, or someone, rather more special than had so far tried. Here at Aintree there was a Turner, an A35 and an A40, an Anglia and four Sprites, their drivers each as determined as the others to break the Delta's victory stranglehold.

Waiting quietly in anticipation on the grid was a young Aussie about to join the queue of hopefuls. This was his first UK race, and sitting in his Sprite, with its untried Weslake head fitted just the night before, he surely must have been wondering whether some of his choices in life had been the right ones. After all, it was less than three months since he had arrived in the UK, four years after leaving home with the express aim of fulfilling his life's ambition to become a racing driver. Now it was a case of put up or shut up, and perhaps – just perhaps – a small chink appeared in the armour of his ironclad confidence as the starter's flag dropped.

The clutch bit deeply, generating lurid smoking wheelspin, and competitors with better traction rapidly shot past, demoting him to a lowly fifth in class. It could hardly be called an auspicious start. And it was, after all, the boss' car, so he'd better not shunt it.

He had not known his boss John Sprinzel very long, but the two would become great mates, or 'matey', as 'Hawks' was prone to saying. He had met the genial head of the Donald Healey's Speed Equipment Division when he answered an advert for a workshop foreman in the *Evening Standard*. He badly needed the job as cash was getting low. Sprinzel was immediately taken by his sense of humour and the fact that 'he had the most colourful choice of language of anyone I knew. I was impressed by Paul's interest in cars, and agreed to give him a trial.'

The new employee soon made his presence felt; not least because he was a capable and hard worker, and on many mornings he could be found bunked up in the garage after a late night's spanner session. This latter behaviour also had the useful side effect of minimizing expenses; an important consideration for a fresh face in the kangaroo valley of London's Earls Court.

Working alongside them in the Grosvenor Street offices was one of a steady stream of Anzacs. 'Greenie' – John Green – had joined Paul as his mechanic for the weekend. They had known each other from their days with the Victorian Amateur Drivers' Club, and after deciding between them that Liverpool was definitely somewhere north of London, had set off the previous day on the 250-mile trip to the Aintree circuit to try their luck. Stopping *en route*, they cut the seats in the Weslake head they hoped to fit before practice, and with Hawkins behind the wheel dicing all the way, they had a rather 'interesting' drive, as 'Greenie' would later understate.

Arriving at 2.00pm, the pair found they had just made it before the practice session closed. With no time to fit the new head, 'Greenie' was quickly deposited as Hawkins sped off to acquaint himself with the circuit, his luggage still rolling noisily and unceremoniously around in the boot!

First event of the Aintree International 200 meeting the following day was the closed car race of 10 laps, for which was entered an eclectic range of machinery in three classes. Elites, Morgans and Sprites would mix it with Jaguars and Astons in a typical build-up to the main event, when Brabham, Moss, Surtees and Salvadori would clash. Jack Sears, in his Aston, was familiar with Aintree, and reckoned that to be quick at the combined horse and motor racing circuit you needed above all to get the apexes right. Aintree would need both respect and precision.

As the race got under way, 'Greenie' had a limited view leaning out from the pits to see along the straight. After the disappointing start Hawkins had made a move further out on the circuit, and the 'Team 221' Sprite was fourth in class as he charged past him in the No 3 pit at the end of the first lap. 'The next must have been a beauty because he came past in third. Rounding the right-hander into the pits straight on the third lap he spun out whilst attempting to pass the Speedwell Sprite but passed us still in third position. On lap four he was right up the Speedwell Sprite's exhaust pipe all the way, hence it spun on the same right-hander and Paul got through into second position.'

Further up the placings, Sears would eventually go on to take the outright win, but 'Greenie's eyes were only for Paul as the little Sprite gamely harried the as yet unbeaten Van Niekerk Delta for lap after lap, pushing him hard into every corner. 'Finally, on the last lap of the last corner, the same right-hander into the pits straight, Paul went past the Delta on the inside – *sideways*. Seconds later he received the chequered flag – we had won.'

They were overjoyed. They had taken not only the 1000cc class first, but class fastest lap as well. Paul collected his £50 prize money, along with £250 from BMC and was immediately signed up by Castrol. He was on his way. It had been a great day, but it was not quite finished yet, and it had a sting in the tail, for as the exuberant pair charged back to Sprinzel in London with the good news, they were clocked by the Law at 90mph and fined the exact same amount as had just been won!

With the Healey family now looking to concentrate on

developing the boat building side of the business, the Speed Division was put up for sale, and though Paul cheekily offered to buy the firm from Donald Healey on numerous occasions, he simply hadn't the cash. Sprinzel, on the other hand, was well placed to take advantage of the potential, eventually purchasing the company and often referring to Paul as his partner.

'Paul was never a real business partner, so that when I bought the business from Donald it was my responsibility, but Paul came along to continue running the workshop and develop the Sprites still further. He was interested in getting race drives, not in getting rich! Even so, we were partners in that although we used a lot of my contacts to get reground camshafts, flowed cylinder heads, etc, and although my experience with the cars went into whatever we did, he had the responsibility for the assembly and tuning of the cars.'

It was both a busy and an exciting period in the young expat's life. There was not only a new city and country to explore, but a whole new set of relationships and culture to go with it, and the swinging London of the early '60s was the place to be. In between building 'ace' cars for friends like Cyril Simson and David Harris, the pair delved deeply into the enormous amount of evening activity.

Partying was big, and the motorsport fraternity tended to split into natural groupings. 'Nobs' could be found at the *Steering Wheel Club*, whilst the 'journos' headed for the *Windsor Castle*, at Notting Hill Gate, and everyone else made for the *Victoria Tavern*, on the north side of Hyde Park. They would say that you could tell when 'Hawks' arrived by the squeal of rubber as his car (or was it one from the garage?) scribed a 180-degree handbrake turn to park. One occasion, so the story tells, there weren't enough glasses to go round at a party, so he grabbed a travel bag and white towel, wandered down to the nearest pub, slipping a towel over his arm and proceeded methodically around the saloon bar scooping up all the empty glasses.

Paul and Sprinzel became good mates. 'We went out most evenings, usually with a small gang of other Oz mechanics who were recruited at the *Down Under Club*. These guys were on the 'big tour' and would generally stay six months or so before returning with the ubiquitous Mercedes to help offset costs', says Sprinzel. 'Paul was an exception as he said from the start that he wanted to get into racing. As he said, he was staying for the long haul.'

Ensconced in the back of the Grosvenor Street showrooms, the 23-year-old Hawkins was soon proving his worth as a first-rate mechanic. By mid-1960 the new firm was in full swing converting production Sprites for race and rally competition, and with the additional responsibility for servicing and preparing the wide range of customer vehicles he was kept more than busy.

Cyril Simson had known John Sprinzel for some time, and along with David Harris they had formed Team 221 to compete at Goodwood in the Easter races of '60. Simson and Hawkins quickly hit it off, and before long the pair struck an agreement. They would share Cyril's car for the longer distance races, which suited the Sprite well, while Paul would drive it in shorter events, undertaking the fettling while Cyril picked up the tab. It was an arrangement which would work well, and Cyril remembers that period with a wry grin, saying: 'Paul was a great personality, and though he spent a lot of his time at the *Down Under Club* getting seriously pissed, he had an absolutely infinite capacity for work as well.'

One example of this hard grafting ability came in June, at the eighth running of the Rouen-les-Essarts Grand Prix, which was being run in two two-hour sessions. Cyril somehow managed to blow the engine in practice, and with the race scheduled for the next day there was nothing for it but to spend a sleepless night rebuilding it in preparation.

With Cyril acting as 'gofer' and sustained by an endless supply of coffee, Paul set to with a vengeance. By 1.00am the thing was in a thousand bits, and by 4.00am there seemed to be another thousand. With the first race due to start at 10.00am, the real race was in completing the engine rebuild and getting it all fitted into the car in time. With 15 minutes left there were still bits all over the show, but somehow they managed to make the grid by the skin of their teeth, with just one lonely bolt holding the starter motor in place. Sadly, all the hard work was in vain and they posted a DNF.

Undaunted, the double-act then moved on to Goodwood, where they took a seventh in class in the Tourist Trophy before heading off to Germany for the ADAC 500 at the 'Ring', picking up some Americans *en route* at Aachen, who kindly offered their help. Cyril remembers that other teams thought them a 'huge joke' with their single set of racing tyres, and just a set of Gold Seal road tyres in case of rain, but the pair still managed a class win, all jokes aside.

Teaming up with John Patten, 'Hawkeye' – as he had now become known – was next off on the rally route, tackling his first RAC Rally. After losing several minutes when they suffered a puncture during the first night, they fought back hard and, aided by Paul's wins on the circuit tests at Mallory Park and Brands Hatch, they took a respectable fourth in class with the Sprite.

'Hawkeye's 1961 season began in style when he set off for his first American adventure in the Sebring 12-Hours. This was a major event for the company, and John Sprinzel engaged the services of Stirling and Pat Moss to ensure a blaze of publicity across both the USA and UK for their newly completed alloy-bodied Sebring Sprites.

Two cars were entered in the preceding day's four-hour GT race. The intention was to race both PMO 200, piloted by Pat Moss and 'Hawkeye', with Stirling driving Sprinzel's S221, and then use the best bits of both for a single entry in the following day's 12-hour endurance race. Clutch problems with Stirling's S221 car prompted Pat to offer PMO 200 to him for the four-hour race, leaving herself and Paul with the limping S221.

In the race itself, Stirling had difficulty staying with the flying Abarths, though with Bruce McLaren close behind, he was pressing hard when the clutch problem struck again. He managed to find the fire extinguisher, though wisely he decided to pit before cooling the plate with it, and rejoined the race still holding on to his fifth place, where he would eventually finish. Pat was also experiencing clutch problems, and came in to hand over to Paul to enable him to save the engine for the following day's 12-hour race. It would not be the last time that his mechanical knowledge would be valued as a means of prolonging the racing life of a car, and with gentle nursing, the sick machine finally managed a reasonable seventh place.

Following overnight preparation, the 12-hour event was comparatively quiet after Cyril Simson parked the little car in a sandbank, taking some time to dig it out before passing it over to Paul. A final 37th overall and fourth in class was the best that could be managed, though echoes of the event had not yet finished with Paul Hawkins.

In the previous day's four-hour race there had been another Sprite entered by Peter Jackson and driven by his close friend Richard Melville alongside Speedwell co-director Graham Hill. Though Peter was in England at the time, Melville, on meeting up with Paul at Sebring, had quickly realized that the Sprinzel operation was the one to become involved with, which is precisely what he advised Peter to do once he had returned to England.

Peter's memories of events of that time are classic. 'I had run my car in a small club event at Brands Hatch and soon realized that in its current state it was not very competitive. Things were hastened by the fact that whilst driving it on the road shortly afterwards the crank broke. So it was a case of bite the bullet and off to Sprinzel to have it converted into a proper Sebring Sprite.

'Paul at this time was in charge of setting up the racing side at Sprinzel, and he was driving one of their cars in most events. Richard and I were sharing a flat on the Cromwell Road, and this soon became a meeting place for the many Australians and New Zealanders who were involved in motorsport at the time. Two ladies of the night held court in the top flat, and any clients had to run the gauntlet of us rowdy lot in the ground floor flat, which always caused much mirth.

'The first international event with the newly refurbished Sprite was at La Châtre, in central France, and as Paul had supervised the transformation of the car he kindly decided to come out and see how we would get on. Richard and I drove down, having taken the cars over the Channel on Silver City Airways, who were still operating in those days, while Paul flew to Paris and hired a Peugeot 403 and drove down separately.

'The weekend started with an organized parade of all the competing cars around the town to put the locals in the right frame of mind, followed by a civic reception at the *mairie*, where there was lots of champagne, etc. Here things started to go a bit sideways when, egged on by Paul, I shot the mayor's glasses off from 20 paces with a champagne cork. This did not go down entirely well, and I think our number was taken at this stage.

'Practice went off well. It was a pretty 'Mickey Mouse' circuit, with a very tight first-gear hairpin about 50 yards from the start. As I was on pole, things looked quite promising for the race next day. However, there was something of a hiccup. That evening we had a pretty wild party, and afterwards, as we wended our way back to the hotel, Paul persuaded me to get into a 2CV van that was parked outside the local *boulangerie* and he and various others proceeded to push it down the road.

'Sadly our progress had been observed and several hefty locals appeared on the scene, whereupon my assistants melted into the night. The next thing my girl friend and I were bundled out of the 2CV and into the local police station and locked up for the night. All requests for bail were in vain. I spent a very sleepless night with visions of Paul standing in for me and driving the car!

'In the end I did get out in time and duly won the race easily. Paul, meanwhile, had a head-on collision with the race director on a narrow lane on the way to the circuit. This was another black mark for our *équipe*, not to mention the fuss when Paul returned the Peugeot somewhat bent and with four bald tyres. I am afraid that we were a pretty wild and badly behaved bunch, but it seemed a lot of fairly harmless fun at the time.'

Back in England, the high rates at the upmarket Grosvenor Street address had by now forced a move into somewhat more affordable premises at Lancaster Mews, where the Hawkins pranks continued unabated. 'The customers needed a very good sense of humour to cope with the practical jokes which were frequently played on them', continues Peter. 'The more posey the customer, the more they were often made to suffer (can't imagine why!).

'We had a good supply of nasty gadgets at the time which came from a very good joke shop in Miami. Favourite was a device which was connected to a spark plug, which when the engine was started lit up with clouds of green smoke and gave off a hideous noise; there were also whistling devices which used to be inserted up exhaust pipes. Needless to say Paul was at the forefront of these exploits.

'He was an absolute hooligan driver on the road at the time and always worked on the theory that if you drove at twice the speed limit it would fool the speed traps. Of course there were a lot of regular customers who brought their cars into Sprinzel's for either regular service or tuning in one way or another, so Paul had a regular supply of unusual cars in which we tended to roar around London, handbrake turns in the middle of traffic being a speciality.

'I remember on one occasion someone brought in an Austin Westminster which was fitted with a police bell. Needless to say, this proved absolutely irresistible to Paul and we had an epic trip down to Kingston-on-Thames to visit the Peel brothers, who were artists in sheet metal work and used to build some of the alloy bodies for the Sebrings.

'On the way down we were going through Hyde Park and came upon the usual traffic jam around the Serpentine. Paul, never one to hesitate, promptly drives around the outside of all the traffic and traffic islands, in the face of the oncoming traffic, bell going full blast! Unfortunately, as we reach the traffic lights, we also meet a policeman on a motorbike, who makes Paul

35

reverse the entire way back! Fortunately, the police had a sense of humour.'

The fun and practical jokes would continue way beyond Sprinzel's, but for now, having acquired a taste for internationals, it was typical of Paul's determination that he decided to undertake some serious professional assessment of his abilities, and in April he headed off to Brands Hatch and the Racing Drivers Training Division of the Cooper Car Company for some observed laps.

Still using Cyril's car, he was again out in mid-year to try his new found skills, but it was Le Mans, where he was paired with Palmolive heir John Colgate in Healey's alloy-bodied Super Sprite, that was to provide the icing on his driving cake that year. He had always wanted to drive the classic sports car circuits, and he was about to achieve one of his greatest ambitions. Unfortunately, the experience was to be short on results, and though they were officially classified as 40th, in fact they had retired after 10 hours with engine problems. Nevertheless, it had proved a worthwhile learning experience as the mental and physical preparation necessary for the 24-hour marathon would prove more than useful on later occasions.

Meanwhile, the hubbub at Lancaster Mews continued unabated and the 'Sprite Gang' by now was generating tremendous interest from a wide range of friends and customers. With the 750 Motor Club's six-hour relay race planned for August (the longest race in the UK at that time), the decision to enter a customer team was quickly taken and Team Sebring was soon formed to compete against a mixed bag of 23 other teams at the Silverstone circuit.

This was a unique race in which the fastest club racers of the time, such as D-Type Jaguars and Lotus-Climaxes, would compete in a handicap race against road-model Jaguars, Healeys, MGs, Minis and even veteran 750cc Austin Sevens. It would be a team effort, and together with 'Hawkeye' and Sprinzel were Ian Walker, David Seigle-Morris, Peter Jackson, Chris Williams and Doug Wilson-Spratt, with John Brown acting as team manager.

Having been given a 36-lap advantage, Team Sebring were thought to have been fairly generously treated by some who had raced against them previously, but rules are rules and a racing advantage is never something to be scorned. At the 1.00pm start there were 24 two-car teams ready to go, and by the halfway mark the Jaguars were leading by a diminishing margin from the Sprites, with the latter circulating 5 seconds a lap faster than the handicapper had estimated.

Just half an hour later the enthusiastic Team Sebring took what was to become an unassailable lead. With Ian Walker circulating in an incredible 1 minute 14 seconds compared to the Big Healey's 1 minute 15 they were fairly flying, and unsurprisingly they went on to take a comfortable first place. Hawkins' exuberant contribution to the effort didn't go unnoticed by Ian Walker. 'I recall how I was impressed with Paul's aggressive but precise driving, and I put him on my mental list of drivers for my forthcoming professional racing team', he says.

Others, too, had begun to notice Paul's straightforward, no-nonsense style, and it wasn't long before he and Mini racer Christabel Carlisle became firm friends. 'I wasn't a real girlfriend. I had to be very careful because of publicity, but I could always trust Paul. He was very kind, and always had a wonderful twinkle in his eye. I remember that he had one of those cars you could sit three in the front, and six of us went up to Henley for the day on one occasion. Some mechanic friends from Sprinzel's and their girlfriends came with us. Imagine – they wanted to go to Henley! – quite different from motor racing. It was a lovely day out.

'He would sometimes put on his accent a bit, just to show that he was a blunt Australian, I think, but he didn't have to try. He was quite a tease, too, and used to make fun of *my* accent, but we were very good friends, and he was great fun to be with. He would sometimes talk about Australia, but he didn't talk about his family a lot.'

This was hardly surprising given the strained relationship

with his father. Surprisingly, Christabel recalls that he didn't swear in her presence which, given his reputation, suggests that he really could be a true-blue gentleman as and when the need arose. Like so many others of that time, he would choose to moderate his behaviour according to selected company.

September was the Nürburgring 500 Kms, and once again the combined works/customer team was out to play, and Peter Jackson was right there with them. 'This race was for GT and saloon cars up to 1000cc, and was the major race of the season for the smaller cars. It was very much the happy hunting ground for Abarth, who used to come up from Italy with transporter loads of cars for all classes, and generally swept the board. However, the Sprites did give them a fright for once, though not before we had a good deal of drama in practice.

'Originally the team was to have consisted of Ian Walker/Paul Hawkins, Andrew Hedges/Robert Kuderli, Peter Clark/Peter Jackson, with Richard Melville entered off his own bat. However, Peter Clark rolled his car in practice, and Richard Melville had a hub break and lost a wheel, bending his car severely in the process. I had taken my car over anyway as it was my only means of transport. While doing a bit of unofficial practice the gearbox had started to expire, so we ended up taking the engine and box out of Richard's car and putting them in mine, thanks in no small measure to Paul, who as always mucked in and sorted us out.'

Race day saw 70 cars drawn up for the Le Mans-style start, and first away by a good 50 yards, much to the embarrassment of the Abarths, was the Walker Sprite driven by none other than 'Hawkeye'. Ian Walker, also acting as team manager on this occasion, picks up the story:

'Paul and I drove my car, but due to fatigue and illness I only did about five laps (of 22) of the old Nürburgring circuit. Paul did the rest of the 500 kilometres and I believe his was the fastest car in our class and helped the team win the coveted ADAC team prize. He was not only a determined, courageous driver, but was also very gritty.'

It had been a good race, pleasing BMC no end, and was in fact one of Team Sprinzel's best efforts. No other British car would finish in the top three of the 500 Kms for another eight years.

In November Paul was off again in Sprinzel's car, though on this occasion with new partner Vic Elford, with whom he would form a lasting friendship. Vic recalls that he and John Sprinzel had entered the RAC Rally, when at the last minute John nailed a factory drive and generously offered the already prepared PMO 200 to himself and Paul.

Calling Paul an 'incredible character', Vic remembers him saying: 'Well you know, Vic, I can't drive at night and I can't navigate, so you're going to have to do all the night driving and the navigating, and I'll sleep at night while you do the driving, and you navigate me during the day'. 'And that's pretty well what happened', says Vic. 'I did all the night driving, he did all the day driving, and I was trying to stay awake for 24 hours at a time!' (Images of Paul's brother doing the penance spring to mind.) It was not to last, however, and at the top of the infamous Horseshoe Pass the Sprite's rear springs and gearbox failed. Even with help from the BMC support team the car stayed busted, and Paul had driven his last ever competitive rally. Though obviously disappointed, it was not rallying that fate had decreed as the future for the young mechanic-turned-driver, and by year's end Robert Paul Hawkins had at last achieved his life's ambition to join a full-time professional racing team. It was to be the newly formed Ian Walker Racing.

Chapter Three

It's now or never

At the beginning of 1962 the Beatles were topping the charts, and Carnaby Street was the place to be seen as stretched British bobbies tried to sort the ever clashing Mods and Rockers. Mods, pressing the boundaries of sartorial elegance to the limit, adorned their scooters with ever more lavish chrome and 'did' the cafe scene, while their opposite number, the Rockers, did their utmost to 'hang out' in scruffies, screaming around the streets on their mean machine motorbikes.

Had he been forced to choose, Elvis Presley fan Paul Hawkins could only have been a Rocker, for it was not just his love of speed in a car or on a bike that singled him out from Joe Average, but his forthright attitude and plain, no-nonsense approach.

Paul's deal with Ian Walker involved drives in the newly purchased Lotus 23 while he continued to spanner away in workshops prepared for the fledgling team. In fact, Ian's entry into 1962 as a team owner/manager brought not just a new team to the arena, but one which was quickly considered to be amongst the most professionally operated racing organizations in the business.

Ian initially established workshops at Fortis Green, later moving to Temple Fortune, and as the team's original full-time employee Paul would soon be joined by other drivers and mechanics demonstrating a dedication akin to his own.

John Pledger, fresh from Team Lotus, would become one of his 'cobbers' bending spanners for Ian. He recalls sharing the same devil-may-care attitude with Paul, saying: 'We hit it off straight away. Paul was just a real lively, bubbly, typical Aussie.'

As chief mechanic, the straight-talking Yorkshireman had the theoretical and unenviable task of trying to keep Paul in line, and at times it must have been a thankless task. 'He was down the workshop every day, but on the 'phone chatting to birds. He used to spend a long time in the office, shoot out, and disappear for a couple of hours; though to be fair, he used to muck in.' And mucking in would soon be the order of the day, as the team quickly expanded to run two Lotus 23 sports-racers alongside its pair of Lotus 22 Formula Juniors.

Paul's first driver outing proved a great success, though not all was as it should have been as Lotus were having difficulty in mating the engine to Ian's specified five-speed gearbox, and the transporter was not yet ready. Undeterred, he designed a quick-fix arrangement and headed north in a borrowed furniture van to give the 23 class honours at Oulton. A fortnight later came a similar win at Goodwood, and as the season progressed, further class wins and fastest laps would become the order of the day as his confidence and competence increased.

Unfortunately, his prowess off the track left just a little to be desired from the point of view of that officialdom which he so loved to hate. Having long since acquired a competition licence to keep his Aussie road licence company, it now only left the small matter of a valid English road licence to think about. He had been driving all around Europe and the UK for the best part of three years, but officialdom was slowly closing in, necessitating that formal piece of paper.

Legend has it that he somehow acquired (don't ask) that most suitable of all learner vehicles, a Ferrari, in which to take his test, which halfway through had the examiner bailing out with 'You're f***ing mad', before storming off to leave him somewhat bemused and perplexed. After all, he *was* a professional driver, and from his point of view, more than competent to manage everyday traffic. Little events such as driving halfway along Oxford Street on the footpath were of course perfectly normal to Paul, who seemed to consider all options fair game, and it was mostly the innocent or the very brave who offered to sit in the passenger seat.

Richard Hudson-Evans was one who took up the challenge, and to this day he vividly recalls that he once drove with him from Hammersmith down the Great West Road past Chiswick to the Cherry Blossom boot polish roundabout at a scandalous, balls-out 100mph in his Willment-modified Zodiac, 'red lights and all – he never lifted once'. It was an outrageous style, which probably accounts for a visit he had one night at their workshop premises at Temple Fortune, where as usual they were burning the midnight oil.

'It was quite late,' says John Pledger, 'because we used to work all night, every night. Temple Fortune was on the main road, but it was around the back of the garage where we had these six or whatever lockups, and the police station was three doors up. The police used to come around quite often 'cos they knew we were working, and have a cup of tea and a fag or whatever, but this one was on duty, and he obviously wasn't from Temple Fortune police station.

He came in, and Paul says: 'Can I help 'ya, mate?'

Policeman: 'I'm looking for Paul Hawkins.'

Paul (calling back): 'Have you seen Paul, John?'

John: 'No, mate, he's gone back to Australia three weeks ago.'

Policeman takes off his hat and puts it on the counter: 'Jeeze, you don't know how lucky that bloke is. There's enough here to put him away for three months!'

'He was so brazen,' continues John, 'he'd get stopped for jumping red lights in London (bearing in mind this was the early Sixties and there wasn't much traffic about). He'd say to the copper: "F*** me, mate, it's gone 12 o'clock. Back home all the red lights stop at 12 o'clock. You just take your chance and go through 'em." And he used to get away with it.'

His Zodiac road car was thought to be ex-*Rallye des Alps*, and it was certainly modified with a four-speed 'box and some heavy-breathing carburettors to help it along. So, with plenty of practice under his belt, it was not entirely surprising that he took Ian's similar car to third place at the Brands Hatch Six Hours, proving to all and sundry that with or *without* a piece of paper, he could drive well enough to dismiss such trifling matters as the Highway Code as irrelevant.

Along with Peter Ryan, Peter Ashdown and Bruce Johnstone, the team was off to the 'Ring in May where between them Ryan and 'Hawkeye' set fastest class lap of just 10 minutes 26.6 seconds before the engine swallowed a rather indigestible piece of carburettor, putting an end to their race. At the time, they had been holding a two-minute lead over their team-mates Ashdown and Johnstone, who stroked their remaining 23 to an excellent eighth overall against the heavy-brigade Ferraris, Porsches and Astons.

Tragically, Canadian Peter Ryan's promising career was to be cut short, and in July, after his fatal accident during a Formula Junior race at Reims, the team would have the unenviable task of rebuilding their confidence and enthusiasm. 'Obviously it was a bad time for us. We were gutted,' says John Pledger, though the demands of the racing calendar left little time for quiet reflection. 'We were so busy,' he continues, 'like, the next weekend we were somewhere else. You just got on with it.' A simple statement, said with feeling, that reflects how much motor racing and death were entwined at that time. It would not be the last time that Paul and his many peers would have to face their mortality.

Just a fortnight later the team would be in Clermont-Ferrand, where Paul was to have an adrenaline rush that was just as unwelcome. The Michelin town's circuit was quite long, twisty and hilly, with numerous access points around its length as the teams practised for the race, and amongst those giving of their best that day was a young David Hobbs. He had come down with his brother Richard, entering his trusty Lotus Elite, while Paul as usual was in the Walker car. David: 'We were going up this fairly steep hill and Paul was coming up behind me in the Lotus 23, which is obviously quicker than the Elite. I had never been one for holding people up, and he was *much* quicker than I was, so I pulled over to the right. He went around the left of me, because we were about to come to a left-hander, so obviously we both wanted to be as far over to the right-hand side of the road as we could, and no sooner had he pulled in front of me than a Simca came down the hill with four farmers in it! I mean...seconds earlier and it would have nailed Paul or me head-on.

'Of course, everyone pulls into the pits, gets out and says: "Did you just see what I thought I saw?" They were just going down to town. They couldn't understand what was going on with all this traffic going the other way at a hell of a speed. Just a bit hairy!' Once the mayhem had settled Paul would go on to practise faster than a Ferrari and Peter Arundell in the works twin-cam, though regrettably a gearbox failure would rob him of a place in the race.

Scary as the event was, there was always the post-race party to look forward to as a means of blowing off steam, one of which found 'Pledge' and 'Hawkeye' in an interesting situation. 'On the Continent at that time after every race there was a big party in the town square or wherever,' says John. 'Everyone was getting pissed,' (except John, who doesn't drink) 'and we were staying in a hotel about 300 yards down from where this party was going on. It got quite late and I said to Paul: "Come on, mate, let's go home". He said: "F*** that, I'm not walking home," so he actually nicked this black DS19. There were no keys in it, but it was all downhill, so he opened the car door, we got in, he's knocked the handbrake off and down we go to the hotel.

'But at all these little parties it was always the mayor of the town giving out the prizes and whatever. It was the mayor's car that he nicked, and the *gendarmes* apprehended us. I think from memory that the police station was just around the corner from the hotel. They took us both there, and of course Paul couldn't speak a word of French, and nor could I, so we just pleaded ignorance and they put us in this room with a desk. And when the *gendarme* puts his hat on it...and there's a window there...Hawkins puts on the hat, and out the window! No-one ever chased us for it or whatever, so he got a *gendarme's* hat as a souvenir.'

By the end of the year, Paul's drives with Ian Walker in both the Lotus 23 and the open-wheeler 22 had guaranteed him a continuing place in the team, and though he had a heart of gold, nerves of steel, dollops of humour and the necessary mechanical 'feel' to coax the best from a car, he would need it all and more to carry him through the challenges he would face in '63.

The recruitment of fellow Aussie Frank Gardner was an excellent move on the part of Ian Walker. He was both quick and experienced, already having won the New South Wales sports car championship before coming to the UK, where he had driven Formula Juniors for Brabham. Ian was pleased that he had somehow tempted him away from Jack, whose Formula Juniors would now replace the Lotus 22s. With his engineering background, Frank not only had a mechanical sympathy akin to Paul's, but the analytical skills that enabled him to develop a car systematically. He also enjoyed a laugh, and the combination of Frank and Paul would often be cause for good fun and occasional outrageous hilarity. In many ways they were birds of a feather, whilst in others totally different. 'I liked them both equally,' says John Pledger. 'Frank was an engineer, and a bloody fine engineer. They were as different as chalk and cheese. Two completely different characters, but both really funny. Frank was a thinking driver, where Paul used to go balls-out.'

And it would show in the results. Both Frank and Paul were now regularly driving the Brabham Formula Juniors, and there is little doubt from the tone of Frank's memories whom he saw as number-one within the team. 'Paul and I were team-mates as such,' he says 'I on the technical side and Paul was the willing hand to do the gofer bits. His application was always willing, helpful and wanting to better himself and the team, plus his driving ability. Paul had been around some interesting people on the rally side, plus all kinds of automobiles, although the channels of life seem to have taken him along the racing car direction.'

Now, confronted by someone who could better him in almost every arena, Paul got into the business of trying harder. And as just about any driver worth their salt will tell you, inexperience and trying harder usually means just one thing – a big off! And that's exactly what happened at Aintree in late April, as Frank took a well-earned second place and Paul had his first big shunt at Tatts Corner. Fortunately he was uninjured, though the car had definitely seen better times.

He was leaving the circuit when he spotted a group of sheilas in a Cortina festooned with Aussie flags, and without any unnecessary preamble, he was off with the speed of a headless chook (chickens to pommies).

'We were just sitting waiting to get into the huge queue leaving the track when there was this shout and a young fella at my driving window saying: "Slip in front of us and we'll meet you at the pub on the right down the road," says Nancy Tonks, or 'Tonksie' as she would be known. She and her friends were 'doing' Europe in the way only Aussies can, and they soon had a friendship brewing. 'We were always ringing and going to the pub, and that's how it was. While Paul and I were not 'ow-you-say, a couple, we were great mates, as it was easy to be with him, but I think because he recognized that I was travelling the world and had absolutely no time for commitments, he was able to relax with me and I think, and felt, I was his surrogate sister. He was as generous as the day was long, despite the aggressive nature of his business, but hugely liked from the boss, Ian Walker down.'

Sharing experiences, they soon discovered a common past, which surprised them both. 'While we were in one of our many talks, we discovered that we must have been at the speedway at the same time because names and drivers and incidents kept coming into it, and one or the other would say: "Yes, I remember that", and he told me that he used to climb over the fence to get in, because his dad was a minister at that time and couldn't afford the money to get in.' (Note: The 10-foot high concrete fences surrounding the Brisbane Speedway/Exhibition ground were topped with broken glass.) 'Dad had seats in one of the stands, the John McDonald it was, and Paul used to rib me unmercifully about being 'little Miss Rich Bitch'. It was so good-natured. He could call you for everything, then smile, sort of like how Aussies say: "G'dday, you old bastard", and it's a complement. He had it down pat.'

Just a fortnight later, Paul was again fending off the opposition, both within and without his own team, on this occasion at Silverstone, taking a third in the Junior and a first in the 23. However, it was a race meeting that would influence him for other, much more personal, reasons.

'Christabel Carlisle had had a wild skid and ended up hitting a marshal,' recalls Nancy. 'As we were driving from the track, even though we were in the line-up of cars, Paul stopped the car, ran over to her, put his arm around her shoulders and said a few words to her.' He returned to the car amid much horn blowing and gesticulating before taking off again. 'He was unusually quiet, and the pair in the back seat were trying to talk as though they didn't know how he felt (maybe they didn't), so I had to tell them to button up,' continues Nancy. 'We pulled into a pub down the road and he just sat with his beer and said almost nothing. It was really sad to see him. It's always a fear that they have that they'll hurt someone unwittingly, and he felt for Christabel. She was such a nice girl.

'When we got back to London that night, we went straight around to Ian's garage where the cars were stabled, and the other two decided to go up to the pub. They asked me, too, but Paul asked me to stay back and he just said to me: "Tonksie, that was something I've always feared, and I could feel her anguish." He was an old softie beneath all the fun and laughter. So much for the aggressive, do-or-die racing driver. People were important to him, and I think that was what drew people to him.'

Another fortnight later and Paul was again pushing his new team-mate hard. This time in France, where Frank Gardner picks up the tale: 'As a driver with the Ian Walker team I can only recall one incident of brain fade, which was the last lap at Montlhéry, when Paul passed me under the brakes backwards and put the car into the wall, doing a reasonable amount of damage. The team was not impressed with the performance.' Nor was team boss Ian Walker: 'I had to have harsh words with Paul, since we were running 1–2, well clear of the rest of the field, and yet Paul was trying his damnedest to overtake Frank, which was stupid from a team point of view.'

Suitably chastised, it was shortly after at Crystal Palace where Paul overcooked his Brabham's brakes, sending it smacking into the circuit wall at a sickening 110mph, and for a third time fortunately coming out unscathed. Luck had been on his side so far. Until Rouen, that is, where again he raced Frank unnecessarily. And again Ian 'had to have harsh words with him and this time with a threat that he would be kicked out if he did it again'.

It wasn't only on the track that the pair of Aussie bucks found themselves competing. Naturally, anything that might provide an advantage would be considered, and the cars' handling was one key area that, if set up for a driver's preferred style, could result in substantial lap time improvements. Their different driving preferences therefore meant that the cars' suspension set-up was an area that received regular and detailed attention from both.

Steele Therkleson was spannering for Ian at the time, and recalls: 'Frank and Paul were always messing around. They were forever fiddling with the handling of the Lotus 23 and Ian got sick of it.' He sent Frank, Paul and John Pledger off to Sweden for a race, then, with the protagonists out of the way, he set about the 23 with a vengeance, and a set of Lotus specifications. Steele continues: 'Ian and I set to work and set one of these 23's up... We found the centreline, measured everything off, and set everything *precisely* to their specifications. We took it down to Brands Hatch and, so we would have an absolutely objective opinion about it, we put Peter Arundell in the car. He did five laps in it and he came in. He said: 'I don't know what you've done to that car, but it is without doubt the best handling 23 I have ever driven. Whatever you do, don't meddle with that set-up'. Ian drove it himself, and he was a very competent driver. We also let Henry Manney, the American journalist, drive it...and Ian, very shortly thereafter, wrote an edict: "Thou shalt not meddle with the handling". In other words, Paul and Frank were told to keep their grubby little fingers off.'

It was proving to be a difficult time for the 25-year-old 'Hawkeye', but his problems weren't over yet, as 'Tonksie' remembers: 'He was a bit reticent with his private life. I know of one girlfriend...both she and her brother Trevor were motor racers. He told me he was really keen on her, almost to the point of thinking of asking her to marry, but found she was seeing a mechanic in another team, so there was a lot of bad blood with that, and he definitely took it out on the team.'

Now, with driving skills in question, his team place in jeopardy, his professional life in turmoil, and his private life in tatters, Paul's confidence and composure were being hard-pressed. However, there was still one more small matter which needed urgent attention. 'Paul as a team-mate was pretty consistent provided you overlooked the villainy that came with the package,' says Frank. 'I recall an irate mother being in the Ian Walker race office accompanied by her daughter. The only problem distracting from a nice looking girl was an enlarged tummy that announced some good six months of pregnancy.

'The mother was a little distraught, as she was unable to locate Hawkins, who was accredited as being the father of this little lot. She thought that it was a bit irresponsible, and when did I think Paul would be back in the country? I responded vaguely and said that I was not his minder, and was sorry that she could not contact Paul. The embarrassing part about the incident was that Hawkins was under the desk, tugging at my trouser during the conversation.' Whilst Paul was known to have laid low with friends on occasions of other personal difficulties, the responsibility implied in Frank's story would later be brought into question when Paul's father would hear of a young lass who was keen to marry a racing driver rather than the mechanic actually responsible for the event, but who knows?

By now, Paul was keeping a north eye open for opportunities in other teams, and following a string of fourth and fifth places his placings slowly began to creep back towards the podium. By the end of the season, confidence restored, he was back on form, taking not only firsts at Snetterton and Oulton in the 23, but a class fastest lap at the Cheshire circuit that would stand for the next six years. A quick look at his racing record that year clearly shows more wins, places and fastest laps in the Lotus 23 than he ever achieved in Formula Juniors, and his time with Ian Walker Racing is well summed up by Ian himself: 'I always expressed the thought that Paul was a better sports or GT driver than a single-seat driver, which I think was borne out by his subsequent career after leaving Ian Walker–Team Lotus. When I think of Paul, I remember him as a little boy who never really grew up. He could be shy and yet boisterous...and was always good for a laugh.'

Paul had matured as a driver in his time with Ian, though perhaps other aspects of his interpersonal skills had yet to catch up, as Ian continues: 'My wife has reminded me that Paul had an enormous appetite and she once made the mistake of allowing him to serve himself from a large dish of *boeuf bourguignon*. Paul was totally oblivious of anyone else around the table and apparently helped himself until there was only two or three spoonfuls left for the rest of us. This was not deliberate, but I think it shows how much of his own world he lived in.'

It also begins to demonstrate his complex character. Nancy Tonks, however, is clear on one aspect of it, as she recalls dragging the reluctant 'Hawkeye' off on what was for him one of the greatest challenges and threats he had ever had to face, and it would require courage far beyond the normal call of duty.

'He actually agreed to accompany me to a concert in the *Royal Albert Hall* one night,' she says gleefully. Was this the same man of whom she says: 'His descriptive Aussie language was part of his appeal, and 'bloody' couldn't possibly have been taken away from him or he wouldn't have spoken'? When he appeared, this 'absolute epitome of the elegant, charming, well-spoken and behaved country squire' entered a world that represented the pomposity he had so often berated, and he must have felt completely out of place. Indeed, it must have been comparable to stepping into the jaws of the social tiger, for this was a man who was rarely seen in anything other than oily overalls, casuals or racing kit. 'He never, ever, let me forget how dashing and how *brave* he had been to go to this concert,' says Nancy.

It was foretaste of other social occasions to come.

Chapter Four

Heard it on the grapevine

A motor racing season during the Fifties and Sixties was a busy time, with racing taking place somewhere in the UK and Europe nearly every weekend as teams and drivers competed in their selected classes. More often than not, it was the same people challenging for honours, and therefore hardly surprising that respect and camaraderie would develop amongst what were essentially a common band of like-minded, achievement-orientated personalities. On the track winning was paramount and all was fair in love and war, whilst off the track both friendships and careers would develop in a myriad different directions.

Jeff Uren was one such individual, and while racing his Anglia in the Fifties he had both competed against and teamed up with John Willment and Ian Walker in their similar cars. 'We would compete for example in the 750 Motor Club's six-hour relay race at Silverstone,' says Jeff. 'We used to call ourselves *Scuderia Frotollo Bendori* – the Throttle Benders Team. And we used to love it. We were involved, if you will, at that time in a friendly and competitive way.

Years later that friendship would engender change. In August 1962, John Willment got the nod that he would be offered a Ford dealership in Twickenham, and as a means of promoting his new venture he turned to his friend Jeff Uren to help him achieve a bit of publicity. Jeff: 'At that stage I was going to run the Ford Falcon team in the Monte Carlo Rally for Ford Detroit' (where Paul would drive a service car). 'John and I had lunch and he said: "Isn't there some way we can get together and do something in racing? You know, run a team?" '

Jeff was convinced that they could win the 1963 British Saloon Car Championship with the Cortina GT, so he went along and put a proposal to Ford's PR and motorsports boss, Walter Hayes. 'He'd only just started then with Ford, and in his proverbial way, with his pipe in his mouth and his feet up on the desk, he listened to it all and he said: "I think we should do that." And so there arrived at Willment's these three Cortina GTs.'

It was a great start for the budding team, who were now in the business of challenging for the championship, but both men remained dissatisfied. 'John and I said this is going to be all right for Ford, but I don't think it's going to make a big enough noise. So to go along with those three Cortinas we ordered a Galaxie from the States.' Willment Racing was now in business, and with South African Bob Olthoff signed up, they soon discovered there was a good deal to be had in his part of the world.

'The Galaxie represented quite an expensive investment, and we needed to make some money,' continues Jeff, so as the trip to South Africa was being finalized, he needed to sort out who was going to drive what, and who better to talk to than his old chum Ian Walker? 'Ian and I did the RAC Rally together; I mean, we were friends, we used to live in each other's pockets, so we knew each other quite well, and I think the boys (Paul and Frank) wanted to move on, so we made way for them to join us once we had started to get ourselves established.'

It was in ways such as this that the wheels within motorsport often turned, and in late October Paul found himself tucked up on a plane headed for South Africa as one of the new crew of Willment drivers. Within days of arriving it was party time as they celebrated mechanic Steele Therkleson's birthday, he too having moved with them from Walker's, and the party atmosphere would set the scene for the next three months.

In South Africa the 'Invasion of the Poms' as it became known was big news, as the size of the Willment team for the Kyalami Nine-Hours race alone indicates. Alongside Paul and Frank were Bob Olthoff, John Whitmore and Jack Sears. Top local driver John Love would also be drafted in, while mechanics Ken Brittain and Steele Therkleson would look after the cars. For Ken and Steele it was a pretty tall order to keep the team's three cars in top fettle, though team manager Jeff Uren had ensured that where possible the three drivers remaining for the full 'Sunshine' Series (Bob, Frank and Paul) would shoulder some of the load. Jeff: 'I would say to my drivers – those who could do it – "You have a mechanical knowledge of the vehicles. You want your vehicles to perform, I therefore want you to take a practical interest in it and want you to get some dirty overalls on, and I want you to mechanic on it".'

Whilst he would ensure that they didn't have to get their hands greasy on race days, the clear expectation was that his drivers would be hands-on developers of their cars. It wasn't always plain sailing, either, as Ken Brittain explains: 'I remember when Paul joined us we had a flaming great row over the way the cars were set up. He was the new kid on the block and we were winning every race we went in, so we took umbrage over the way he came and muscled in, but when we got to South Africa he was a different bloke and he apologized for his horrible behaviour. He was great.

'After falling out with him he got his sleeves rolled up and was with us blokes all the time. He'd come and give us a hand to set the car up because he'd want it set up his way (shades of his time at Walker's), and I have to say that I learned a lot from Paul and Frank about setting up single-seaters. When every joint is adjustable where do you start? Pretty logical stuff like stringing things up and measuring datum points and things like that; and just taking a lot of time over it. And when the car goes out it handles straight out of the box.'

They would need to, for the local opposition was no

pushover, and even though the team had the Galaxie available, along with a 289 Cobra and a Lotus Cortina, the latter was vulnerable. Bob Olthoff: 'We had three cars and three drivers and we would swap from race to race. We would drive different cars because the two winning cars were the Cobra and the Galaxie, and the Lotus Cortina was up against some heavy opposition in South Africa so nobody wanted to drive it. I was in charge, so I said: 'OK, right, in that case we'll each just drive a different car in a different race.'

It was a great time for all as they toured the country, leaving the grey skies of an English winter behind them, enjoying the glorious weather, water skiing and sunbathing as they picked the fruits of their local fame. 'It was just brilliant. We were treated like royalty,' recalls Ken Brittain, reflecting the views of all who were there, whilst at the same time hinting that they were also treated to pleasures of a more personal kind.

Paul of course was in his element. Here was a place that both reminded him of his sunshine-filled youth, and offered female company in abundance. He loved it, and would return year after year. In this first year, however, there was a bit of a downside, as Ken continues: 'The thing that amazed me is that he used to get drunk out of his skull every night, after practice, whatever, and he'd be in the car the next morning ready to race. You couldn't get away with it nowadays. His skin used to be between red and purple when he got in the car. Got a bit of a sweat up, like he was going to die. I said: "Paul, you're going to have to cut back." God, he used to knock it back.'

And the Nine-Hours race prize-giving at the *Golden Sands* night club outside Johannesburg was a good example. Ken continues: 'We all bought water pistols. Some of them had wind-up handles on them like starter motors, and they were quite powerful. They had a 50 or 60 foot jet of water. Unbelievable! It got to this prize-giving and John Whitmore was up for something and he put on a so'wester and plastic mac, because we'd already showered everyone else. We all had these guns. God, it was unbelievable. We were the only team that did

A little liquid refreshment at the Jo'burg night club.

it. Completely out of order, and this was a lovely club: beautiful. They had fitted carpet everywhere apart from a little area for dancing.

'They started off firing some water, and then it got totally out of hand and people were getting drenched instead. I can remember someone's wife got so fed up with it she picked up a jug of water and threw it over us. And so it started a free for all in this club, and after these water pistols (or water cannons more like), it became a water fight with jugs of water, so that was it! Now Paul wanted to do one better. He goes out of the main part of this club and got the fire hose, uncoiled it, said: "Right-oh, you bastards" and turned the tap on. I kid you not, there must have been three inches of water from one end to the other. The carpet was floating. Completely wrecked the evening. Absolutely zapped the place.'

At Bulawayo he would again manage to drink rather more than was prudent, though whether it was simply the booze speaking or his natural talent for calling a spade a shovel remains unclear, as Ken recalls: 'He got up to collect the cup. And Paul liked a drop of the old hard stuff, always rat-arsed. You couldn't talk to him after seven o'clock at night. He got up and said: "Thanks for the prize", and then he said: "Call it a race circuit? It's more like a track for mountain goats".' As the civic dignitaries winced with embarrassment, even his own team groaned: 'Oh God, he's off again', says Ken. 'We all just cupped our heads in our hands.'

Any way you looked at it, the series had been a brilliant success for the Willment team, and Paul, though still learning his trade, had come away with a good handful of silverware. Ken: 'He was never the best driver. I mean, he couldn't get a time out of a saloon the way Jack Sears could for instance. People like Jack Sears could drive anything fast and drive through all its problems, but you've got to understand Paul, and if you could set the car up properly and the way he wanted it, he could get a similar time out of it. He wouldn't tolerate a car that wasn't set up properly.'

Back in Britain, Paul more often than not was driving the Lotus 23, though there were to be plenty of Formula Two drives to be had with their ex-Winklemann Lola-Cosworth T55, whilst occasionally he was obliged to punt a borrowed and generally uncompetitive Alexis originally borrowed from Bill Harris, and the results showed a clear difference. Whilst the Alexis generally languished out of the placings in sixth or eighth, the little Lotus was being pushed into useful places, one of which saw him at Silverstone, where his South African motorcycling mate Paddy Driver remembers the post-race party with a chuckle.

'They had a big marquee there, and I remember there was a bit of a wind blowing that night, and there was a guy in a kilt who climbed one of the poles and people were egging him on. Anyway, Hawkins said: "Come with me," and I said: "Where are we going?" He said: "We're going outside. Were going to have some fun. Help me to loosen all the guy ropes." This bloody big tent, I promise you, was floating backwards and forwards, and everybody was so drunk inside, as the tent came over the top of them, they all leaned forward with the tent, and when it moved the other way they all went backwards.'

When the police arrived to see what all the fuss was about, they were soon surrounded by interested partygoers, the instigators thinking it prudent to assist in their inquiries. Paddy: 'We surrounded this poor old copper...and we're busy unscrewing the valves on the tyres!' Unsurprisingly: 'They put their tails between their legs and buggered off.'

Ken Brittain and Paul, having formulated a friendship that would stand the test of time (and quite a few beers), now set to looking at the Cobra before addressing the ADAC 1000 Kms at the Nürburgring. This was right up Paul's street, as for preference he would avoid 'tin tops'. Ken: 'The AC Cobras had a transverse leaf spring, and in order to get the camber right you had to re-roll the eyes of the spring, but it wasn't until Paul came on the scene that we started to look at these cars objectively and see what a piece of shit they were. We worked quite a long time on the back end of these cars and made up some eccentric bolts that went through the centre of the spring so you could turn it round and at least get the cambers the same.'

Whilst the theory was fine, it was going to be up to Paul and his oppo Bob Olthoff to demonstrate its value in the race. In practice it simply piddled it down, and Frank Gardner wasn't too keen on going out in the other Cobra. Jeff Uren did his stuff as team manager and insisted, only to have Frank return to the pits having parked the car upside-down in a ditch, saying to Ray Jones and the assembled crew: 'I'm sorry about that, guys, but you can't aim this thing within six foot of a shithouse door if you've got diarrhoea.'

Fortunately, on this occasion at least, neither South African Bob Olthoff nor Paul suffered similar indignity and the former remembers his team-mate with obvious relish. 'His driving ability, there was nothing wrong with, he was quick. The Cobras were not easy motorcars to drive. Paul didn't mind driving them because they were interesting. He wanted nothing to do with saloon cars. He wanted to drive only open-wheelers and quick sports cars.' In practice the pair set similar times, but it is the race itself which Bob remembers for good reason.

'In the Le Mans start I had a fire. When it started up the carburettors caught fire, and normally they swallow it, so I sailed down the road to the first bend, but the fire wouldn't go out. It had come out of the carburettors and we had great big fuel lines there. I was stopped going into the south bend, and of course you're not allowed to work on the car with outside assistance or tools. You're supposed to be carrying the tools on you. So after the Germans had sprayed fire extinguisher all over me, all over the car, all over everything, I walked back to the pits and then Paul came back with me. We both had pockets full of tools, wrenches and whatever, and we got the car running again. We finished the race in the end. We were third in the class, but we'd lost two laps or something in the process of getting the thing fixed up again.' It seemed that the eccentric bolts had done the job, provided your carburettors didn't catch fire!

Willment cars by now were racing virtually every weekend with very considerable success, and as the team raced across both the UK and mainland Europe, Jeff Uren continued to shoulder responsibility for the operational effectiveness of not just the teams cars, but their transport, refurbishment, preparation and sponsorship. The same was also true of his drivers, and though on the surface all was well, there still remained some unfinished business between Paul and Frank.

Jeff: 'They were a little bit at odds, but that used to be the case with Bobby Olthoff as well. They used to be the best of friends on the surface, but they would, mildly speaking, drain the odd drop of blood from the other's throat if they could. Certainly they did get a bit cool on each other, because I think they were in search of their own separate glory. They weren't there to promote Australia.

'One example of it was that we took two Formula Two cars down to Pergusa – Enna – in the middle of Sicily, and we raced them one weekend as Formula Twos and the following weekend as Formula Ones. I could see the way they were conducting themselves and I said: 'We're going to win this race. Whoever is in the lead two laps from the end stays there, and I want no competition.' And, of course, on the last bloody lap they tried to out-fumble each other and lost the race to the third man, who went through and won it. They were doing things like that, and I told them it was bloody stupid. We had a tremendous amount of Ford sponsorship on that. Going out there, Ford of Italy looking after us and paying all the hotel bills, and arranging dinners for us. We had all the press there, and then they go and do something stupid like that. I wasn't happy. No, no, I definitely wasn't at all happy. And they knew it.'

The team were backed not only by John Willment's Ford dealership, but by Ford themselves, and though the blue oval officially supported Colin Chapman's lithe Lotus cars, they were also interested in ensuring that Colin stayed competitive, as Jeff recalls. 'Sometimes it's very difficult when you're backing somebody officially to be totally honest about what you're doing with other people. But it does help to keep people 'honest'. For example, when Colin was running the Lotus Cortinas and Jimmy Clark was driving it, we were the only team to ever beat Jimmy in the works car. That was keeping them 'honest', and Wally (Hayes) liked that. He thought, quite unofficially, that if you can stir somebody into doing something bigger and better, so much the better.'

Certainly, Ford's support for Willment was considerable, and Steele Therkleson echoes Jeff's view: 'It was really the Ford Motor Company's back-door racing team in England, and as such there was no shortage of anything. If we crashed a car at a race on Saturday, when we got to work on Monday there was generally a replacement car waiting on the forecourt ready for us to make another one. At one stage we had 22 cars. A very successful team.'

Paul, of course, benefited from the arrangement, and contacts made during his period with Willment would work to his advantage in later years, particularly given his outgoing and gregarious nature. 'It wasn't just a question of driving', says Jeff. 'We were involved with Ford over here (UK) and Ford on the other side (USA), and lots of people met people and talked to people whilst these things were going on, and whilst Paul was through Willment's a contracted driver...so he was indirectly a Ford-contracted driver and would get involved in other things. I mean, lots of things happened like that.'

Certainly Paul's time with Willment was productive, and by the end of the season his drives in the Lotus 23 had accumulated sufficient points to warrant a second placing in the *Autosport* Championship, though again, Ken Brittain wasn't impressed with his road driving, which hadn't improved at all. 'He drove like a complete and utter lunatic. Nothing would stop him apart from a train in the middle of the road. He used to keep barrelling on; quite terrifying, really. I mean, he'd spin and just carry on again and he'd still be talking. You didn't queue up to sit next to him.'

Nor had his behaviour improved, for he had discovered a new trick in South Africa concerning paper bags, rubbish bins, oxygen and acetylene. The end result, as mechanic Mike Brown recalls, was that there would be one hell of a bang at all hours of the night 'and the dustbin lid would go a hundred feet into the air.'

Now, to wind up the 1964 season, it was time to head back toward South Africa. With the Galaxie, Cobra Daytona and four-cylinder Formula Two Brabham BT10 in place, they were soon fully prepared for the first race of the series at Kyalami, where the nine-hour endurance race had by now become quite a feature, and consequently much tougher as the years progressed. Bob Olthoff joined Jack Sears in the Cobra coupe, while Frank and Paul teamed up in the Galaxie. Their race would be shortened by a blown cylinder head requiring a massive four hours to fix and any chance of a place was totally gone for a burton. No matter. Following repairs the pair went back out anyhow, just to add the colour of the big booming bright red Ford, as it made up the number to the delight of the huge 60,000 crowd that had come to see the spectacle. While the Cobra managed a creditable fifth, it would be David Piper in his Ferrari 275 LM who would, for the third year running, take the champagne home.

Bulawayo's James McNiellie circuit was next in the queue, just a few days later and the best part of 500 miles distant. This time it was Willment's turn to show a clean set of rubber to the opposition, and whilst Bob Olthoff took the GT class in the Cobra, Paul would win the Rhodesian GP in the Brabham, setting a new fastest lap in the process, before going on to win the saloon car race with another class fastest lap in the Galaxie for good measure. At which point it was party time.

Jeff Uren: 'When he won the Bulawayo Grand Prix, as it was called, it was regarded as a pretty big civic occasion, and these sort of things were celebrated in rather good style, you know. They had parties in football grounds and the public would all come and watch the drivers drinking and collecting their prizes, and that sort of thing. When Paul went up, he went up with a pint of beer in his hand, and when the Mayor of Bulawayo said nice things about him, Paul was embarrassed, so he poured the pint of beer over him. He probably had more than one or two pints inside him.'

Naturally, he wasn't the most popular import of the day, but sobered up and free of the social commitment he abhorred, he and Bob set off for a few days' rest and recreation, heading for the Zambezi river and the Victoria Falls with mechanic Mike Brown. Whilst Mike's following story is representative of some of the antics they got up to, it is worth reflecting a moment on Bob Olthoff's comments about their attitudes to life and death at that time.

Bob: 'We were sort of just living from day to day. It won't happen to me, kind of attitude. I'm too good. I'm too tough. Paul thought very much the same way. In the Sixties he didn't care much for what was going to happen in the future. It was a day-to-day thing,' as Mike's story of the 150-mile run up to the

Falls verifies.

'In those days it was a dirt road. He and Olthoff, driving through the night at 100mph on a little switchback road through the trees, would flick the lights off and count, seeing who could keep in the darkness the longest. Then we got to Vic Falls, and went up the Zambesi water-skiing. Olthoff came off the skis, and it was just like watching Jesus Christ run across the water. There were crocks there!'

Bob picks up the story in his broad South African accent: 'The most dangerous thing really was not crocodiles but hippos. Because a hippo goes underwater like a submarine and he sees the shadow above him, he thinks it's another hippo he's got to attack, so he launches himself off the bottom of the river, hitting the bottom of the boat. Then, of course, people fall out and you get bitten. When a hippo bites, you don't live to tell the tale.'

What Bob neglects to mention is that they had intentionally lengthened the tow rope so, as the hippos rose to investigate,

Hippo-dodging on the Zambezi – water-skiing Hawkins-style

the hapless skier was obliged to aim between the rapidly surfacing mammalian mountains! The intrepid trio now headed back down-river to the Victoria Falls, where all the rocks were worn smooth with the passage of the river over the years, and it was possible to jump in the water like a water slide a good quarter-mile back from the falls. 'Of course, it was the chicken who got out first', says Mike, whilst of Paul he adds: 'He was just bloody wild.' It certainly seems from his actions that Paul, as Bob suggests, simply regarded life as a day-to-day thing, for living till it overflowed.

Mike was the only Willment mechanic on this trip, spending most of his time with Paul as they based themselves at the Olthoff's family home just outside Johannesburg. 'We hired guys out there to help me with the four cars,' he says, adding: 'British team coming out to do the whole Springbok series. We were treated like celebrities.

'On a Friday night they had a Wimbledon-type dirt track in Jo'burg, which we used to go to, and they invited the cars and the team along and did demonstrations by starting off at opposite sides of the track. Paul had the Galaxie and Bob Olthoff had the Cobra, but Paul was determined to catch him in this bloody Galaxie round this track. He got closer and closer, and in the end Olthoff went off and stuffed the Cobra in the wall. There were loads and loads of police there, but they never left the stadium that evening 'cos Paul had gone round all the motorbikes, taken the plug caps off, wrapped up little balls of paper and put all the caps back on. So all these coppers are standing there cranking their motorbikes over, and none of them would start.'

Naturally, the team stayed in hotels as they travelled the country from north to south following the season's racing, and Paul was once again able to capitalize on their minor celebrity status. Mike: 'He was a real womanizer, and quite often wouldn't be back at night. Six o'clock one morning he comes bumbling in with some girl. I said: "It's a bit late to come in, or a bit early isn't it?" So he said: "I've been in the hotel all night.

I got back in at midnight last night. Just picked a key off the board and found myself a couple of rooms. I'm a little worried that they might start cleaning the rooms".

Jeff Uren, meanwhile, had been made an offer he could hardly refuse, and stood to make a few pounds by taking a Formula One car to South Africa. 'So I bought Jo Siffert's Brabham-BRM plus a spare engine, and got Graham Hill to drive it', he says. This was a V8-powered BT11 which, with transport difficulties, made it just in time for the December 12th race at Kyalami, where Graham faced heavy opposition including Lotus' Mike Spence and Jim Clark's replacement, Jackie Stewart, making his Formula One debut. Bob Anderson was there, driving Dickie Stoop's D W Enterprises V8 Brabham-Climax, whilst Tony Maggs failed to start his Parnell Lotus 25 after breaking a camshaft.

The Rand Grand Prix would be over two 25-lap heats, and Paul placed his four-cylinder Brabham on the second row of the grid for the first round. It was something of an eventful race as Hill forged his way through the pack from the rear of the grid, while Paul chased Mike Spence at the front of the pack, and Pieterse managed to flip his Lotus 22 over the rear wheels of the car in front, pirouetting a perfect 180 degrees to face the opposite direction as the grid sped away. Graham would eventually catch Paul in second place, and overtake Spence to take the lead, demoting Paul to a well-earned third.

Heat Two from Paul's point of view would be a punch-up between himself and Bob Anderson, the latter's newer and more powerful car pushing him into fourth as Stewart took first, Hill second and Mike Spence spun off; but it was aggregate times that were to count, and Paul would claim second place behind Graham Hill for a Willment 1–2.

With the South African Grand Prix moved to January, and now the first of the new Formula One season, Frank Gardner was slotted into the V8-powered BT11 Hill had used for the Rand Grand Prix, while Paul retained the four-banger BT10, noticeably down on power when compared to the eight and 12-

cylinder cars. As usual the pair were out to race hard. 'In a way it was a shame that he and Frank were in the same team. They always raced each other before they ever raced anyone else', says Mike, and by now there wasn't much to choose between the aspiring pair, for their fastest race times would be identical to within a tenth of a second.

However, their attitudes toward each other were by now, if anything, even cooler, having spent the best part of two years together, and one unconfirmed story tells of a falling-out between them over a missing manifold. Certainly others of the team had noticed a change in the relationship, and 'friendly rivalry' was now much more about the latter. 'The two of them were inseparable, then they fell out,' observed Ken Brittain.

The grid for the Grand Prix had been limited to 20 places, and with the Formula One circus taking up the majority of the grid, there were just four places left for the remaining 15 aspirants, including Paul, who were required to better 1.37 on a track he had previously described as 'a jolly good go-kart circuit'. It was typical that he would try to pull something out of the hat, and that's exactly what he did.

Mike recalls: 'He went and spoke with Brabham and geared the 1500 TC up and asked Brabham if he could do a few laps so Paul could get on the back of him for a tow; and I think he did a lap that was three seconds quicker than anything else.' At 1.33.1 it was not only well within the required time, but fastest of the 15, and quicker than Siffert and South African Champion John Love, who had been guaranteed a start. Perhaps more importantly, he was within three-quarters of a second of Frank's V8.

The rest of the grid read like a who's who of Formula One, with four World Champions in Hill, Brabham, Clark and Surtees alongside a string of others with huge futures including Spence, Rindt, Gurney, Stewart and McLaren. It was a class field.

There was a clean start, and by the end of the first lap Paul held position with only Siffert between himself and Frank. Up front it was a Clark runaway from start to finish as he lapped the

East London circuit for the first time at over 100mph and his competition began to evaporate with problems from the halfway mark.

Bonnier would need to pit, dropping back considerably, while Anderson, Gurney, Love and Bandini all succumbed to difficulties, which had Paul steadily moving up the board. Lap 60 and Frank pitted to replace a broken alternator belt, only to find none available and he was obliged to complete the race on a replacement battery, though the damage had been done. The consistency, smoothness and reliability Paul had now developed paid off, and he would finish ninth behind Brabham, while Frank had slipped 12th. And that really would have put a smile on his face.

A week later Paul once again returned to East London for the Cape South Easter Trophy, where on this occasion he would win the double-header race from John Love's Cooper, but the wheels within wheels to which Jeff Uren had referred were once again turning, and Paul by now was well known to Dickie Stoop. On at least one occasion, though, they had mixed in somewhat unusual circumstances, as Bob Olthoff recalls.

'We went to the Wangi game reserve, and I had Paul Hawkins, John Whitmore and Dickie Stoop in the car with me, and of course Wangi is known for its elephants. There was a clump of elephants standing a little way into the bush. I was driving the car and Hawkins and Whitmore got out to get closer to the elephants to take photographs. But they didn't see there was an elephant on the other side of the car. When they looked round there was this big bull elephant coming at the car, and I decided there is no way...I'm going! I *know* elephants and motor cars. I dropped the clutch and Hawkins and Whitmore dived in through the back window.'

It seems that not only was South Africa great fun, but you could end up falling on top of your new sponsor as well.

Chapter Five

Wheels of fire

Never a shrinking violet, Paul would often charm friends and acquaintances with his earthy Antipodean expressions. They were as natural a part of his character as breathing, and as his broad accent grated questionably upwards at sentence end, listeners could usually expect a 'Hawkeye special' regardless of company. 'See me coming round that corner? Me arms were goin' up an down like a whore's drawers at a pile driver's picnic.' By the beginning of 1965 journalists were beginning to take note of his rough and ready frankness, and had come to expect not only a good track performance from him, but a newsworthy headline as well.

He was well up to the task, and there were to be numerous occasions when his quick quip and bawdy repartee were as widely reported as his successes and occasional unexpected exploits. By today's standards he could never be called politically correct, and even by the standards of the time he courted disaster as he stomped hob-nailed boots through the thin ice of decency, whilst displaying such huge glowing character and personality that those around him not only forgave his lack of tact, but frequently wished they'd the guts to say it themselves.

The process of Paul's rise to fame for what were sometimes all the wrong reasons had already been launched in South Africa, where he'd not only won the Rhodesian Grand Prix and the first South African Formula One National Championship in the Willment car, but attracted the attention of Dickie Stoop who, already supporting Bob Anderson, was also in the process of developing a privateer challenge for the forthcoming Formula One season. He now offered Paul a deal. Having won the South African race in a Brabham, discussions on the choice of car were somewhat one-sided from Paul's blunt point of view, but as it was Dickie who was putting up the money, it was in the end not so much a discussion as a *fait accompli*, and the ex-Jim Clark Lotus 33, chassis R8, became his new wheels.

Jimmy had severely shunted the car into some straw bales at Aintree the previous year, but after repairs it was now ready and rolling for Paul's next Formula One outing at Brands Hatch in March, where he had an inauspicious start, failing to finish. Following closely were further familiarization races in England until finally deciding it was time to take the D W Racing Enterprises Lotus and Paul Hawkins into the big time. And the big time didn't get any bigger than that mecca of all Formula One races – the *Grand Prix de Monaco* and its 100 laps of Monte Carlo's famous street circuit. 'Might as well start at the top,' as Paul might have said.

Race day was dry and overcast as the team lined up the bright green Climax-engined car on row seven for the start, and though he had suffered an unhappy practice and wasn't content with the handling of the car, he was soon lapping consistently, if not exactly up with the leaders. By lap 79 he was in ninth position and exiting the harbour front chicane when, in his own words, the car 'turned out to sea', spinning and hurtling through the straw bales before diving backwards into the yacht-littered water. His good friend and later partner Jackie Epstein, son of the sculptor Sir Jacob Epstein, picks up the story.

'Now Paul was an excellent swimmer, but being a bit of a case he settled on the bottom in clear water about 30 feet down. The Monaco authorities had thought something like this might happen, so they had a boat with frogmen cruising up and down. They threw themselves over the side and swam down to Paul, who was getting himself out of the cockpit. As this guy got down to him, the first thing Paul did was grab the mouthpiece from the frogman and stick it in his own mouth, take several deep breaths and shoot to the surface – leaving this frogman spluttering at the bottom.'

It was a world news event which paralleled Alberto Ascari's Lancia dip some 10 years earlier, though it was the later release of the John Frankenheimer film *Grand Prix,* starring James Garner, which would enshrine Paul's escapade for all time. In it, Garner's character Pete Aaron can be seen catapulting spectacularly from the circuit into the harbour. From then on, Paul could be heard saying that the scene was based on his escapade; which he would be pleased to repeat for the director should he ever need it!

Rarely reported, however, was that even in the throes of misjudging the chicane and dealing with the errant car as it slid at speed toward the straw bales lining the harbour, his mind was working overtime. Aware of the damaging potential of an overheated engine about to meet the waiting waters of the Mediterranean, he still remembered to hit the 'off' switch; a fact confirmed that night when the car was dragged from the drink, its engine internals completely undamaged. Having watched the remainder of the race from the deck of a nearby floating gin palace, G & T in hand, his later comment was a typical: 'That's one way to cool one's ardour'. Later that year Dickie's Lotus, chassis R8, would be sold to MGM for filming (you guessed it) *Grand Prix*. Both car and event would be recorded for posterity.

Mike Brown, who had followed Paul from Willment as his mechanic, well recalls 'a little bit of a problem' shortly after as he dried out the Lotus in preparation for the following British Grand Prix. There was much to be done, not least of which involved the testing necessary prior to the race. Meanwhile, Paul had decided to swan off on a Formula Two race, angering Mike and prompting him to ask: 'What are you doing – Formula One or Formula Two?', somewhat setting the scene for a showdown. Paul's reply was a typical: 'Well, you go test the car.'

Mike promptly wrote the thing off, which explained why a week later *Autosport* simply stated that Paul's car was missing from the BGP line-up, and 'had unfortunately been pranged by a mechanic during earlier trials'.

Repaired yet again, the Lotus was out in August for the German Grand Prix at the Nürburgring and, as usual, money was tight. Mike: 'We were never wealthy doing Formula One on our own. We'd actually gone back to (Ian) Walker's in a funny way in that we'd nicked a bit of Walker's old workshop to do the F1 car.'

As usual, Paul's pragmatism would shine through in the face of adversity, as Mike recalls: 'He was into selling leather coats and things. He'd always got a bundle on the back seat,' and generating a little bit of black economy income was certainly one way of keeping the wolf from the door, though he also managed some economical savings when it came to accommodation. 'Coming down of a morning he would greet everyone with a flashing smile and bright "Good morning" before walking out of the hotel and driving off, having previously thrown his case from a first floor window! Obviously, the level of the sport was higher than both he and I had time or money to deal with properly,' concludes Mike.

In the race itself Mike would offer his support in a novel manner. 'The car bottomed out. It ground the hose clip away and he lost water and stopped on the circuit. Being rally orientated, I get in the truck and drive all the way round on the gravel track until I find him. He said: "There's nothing we can do with it. We don't want to destroy the motor." Then he asked Mike to stay with the car in case people started pulling bits off. 'So I sit by the side of the track and along comes Gurney and breaks down in his Brabham. He's got the same Coventry Climax engine, so I take the spark box off my car and get Gurney going again. Then a little later, somebody else breaks down (it was Amon, also in search of a spark box). It was like a train of Formula One cars, and this was their out-in-the-country pit lane.' Perhaps he should have charged!

It had not been the most successful of Formula One experiences. Of his four starts in the DW Enterprises car, Paul had achieved two 10th places and two DNFs, including a good dipping. Other races at Spa and Silverstone had been non-starters while the car was being repaired, and it was time to move on. With no team money to support him, he was again a free agent, though starting money was still available if he could cadge a drive. Which is where David Baker stepped in.

As team manager for the Midlands Racing Partnership, he was running three Formula Two cars for '65. MRP had become the Lola works team in '63, when the breeding ground for Formula One had been Formula Junior, and with the advent of Formula Two in '64 they now found themselves with two new T60 monocoque cars, and a converted spaceframe T55 Formula Junior as their third car. With team founder Richard Attwood and BRM number two Richie Ginther as regular drivers, Paul was offered a ride, enabling the team to maximize their opportunities.

David: 'When it turned into Formula Two in 1964, the French had a big championship. There were five races...almost like mini Grands Prix. I think it was at Rouen...Paul hadn't got a drive, but he was there and we'd got a car without a driver. I remember it distinctly, because he wasn't down as the original driver. When the organizers saw he was racing they let him start, but then they wanted me to pull him in and take him out of the race. Well, I refused. They didn't want to pay any money out and I had a job to persuade them at the end.'

Paul would drive for MRP on several occasions, and though more often than not he was in the older T55 he won praise both from David and from Paul Watson, in *Autosport,* who said of his drive at Karlskoga: 'A word of praise should go to Paul Hawkins, who drove an old car, basically a 1963 Junior, and with only a five-speed gearbox instead of everybody else's six. He lapped in 1 min. 27.6 secs. in practice and at the finish of the race was not all that far behind Attwood's newer car.'

With the end of the European season in sight, he could have

been in trouble had it not been for two separate but related facts. The first involved success in sports cars that he might have wished for in Formula One, whilst the other would concern a chance meeting.

Back in March, Paul had managed to hit the press (and upset a few people) yet again with typical subtlety as he practised for Sebring with Warwick Banks. They were to drive an Austin-Healey 3000 in the 12-hour race, a car of which Paul had considerable experience from his days in Australia. Practice was the usual thrash, though it wasn't long before Paul pitted with his somewhat pithy comment on the car's handling. 'Driving this thing is like trying to have sex with a fat woman in a hammock.' Needless to say, it didn't go down too well with some people, though a class win was sufficient reason for Donald Healey to offer a drive in the forthcoming Targa Florio.

In fact Donald could have chosen any number of drivers, but not only did he appreciate Paul's ability, but he also respected his forthright and blunt nature. The pair had locked horns some years earlier, and Paul's determination to face the 'old man' fair and square had led to his promotion at the time. Donald liked people who said what they thought, and the fact that the pair respected each other meant not only a continuing relationship, but solid drive offers over several years.

The Targa was arguably the world's oldest motor race; and without doubt *the* most famous if you happened to be talking to a Sicilian at the time. Over 44.7 miles of rugged scenery, the track wound tortuously over two mountain ranges, passing through the picturesque northern villages of Sicily for 10 long laps. Nearly a quarter of a million locals would cram the route from all kinds of vantage points, yelling themselves hoarse for their heroes: Vaccarella, Bandini, Scarfiotti – or whichever other Italian it was – clothed in a few hundred horsepower of Ferrari red as they flew past them.

Teamed with Monte Carlo-winning rally ace Timo Makinen in an old reconnaissance Healey 3000, supported by Abingdon's rally mechanics, they were the only British entry in the

2000–3000cc category facing a sole Lancia Aurelia Spider and no less than five of the best of Enzo Ferrari's now fabled GTOs. There was little doubt who the locals would be supporting.

The Healey, wearing triple Webers on its alloy head, was tuned for 195bhp, good enough for 125mph in overdrive top, which meant giving little away to the GTOs over such winding terrain, with just a single six-kilometre straight on the whole of the course. Acceleration, handling and reliability would be the key mechanical issue in this famous race, whilst course knowledge would be the paramount driver factor.

With a practice time of 45.31, the Healey was still nearly a minute off that set by the fastest of the GTOs, though of some concern was the effect the exuberant sideways style of the drivers was having on tyre wear. They would need to pit every two laps to replace the rears, and logic therefore dictated simultaneous driver changes. Timo would start, leaving Paul to complete laps three, four, seven and eight.

It was typical Targa time as Sicilian tempers frayed and the organizers concluded that the Healey would be excluded unless it wore its pukka bumpers, now languishing back in England. Spotting a Healey in the parking lot, Paul left an appropriate note on the windscreen and soon afterwards the race car wore a set of bumpers provided by its Aussie owner, proud to have been of assistance.

At the start chaos seemed to reign, though out of the mayhem the race started pretty much on time, sending away first the production cars, followed by the faster GTs and prototypes, at 30-second intervals. Timo streaked away from the start and by lap three, with Paul now behind the wheel, they were lying third. As the GTOs succumbed to failure and accident, the big Healey climbed to lead the class by lap six. On lap seven Paul took the big Healey out again, planning to hand over to Timo at the end of his tour, but the pit crew were aghast to see him stop after just one lap with a serious misfire. The plugs were rapidly changed and he was again on his way, but the problem persisted and a mile up the road Paul stopped.

He tracked the problem down to a cracked rotor arm and ran full pelt back to the pits he had just left, clutching it in his hand, only to be told they didn't have a spare, but that there was one with the spare distributor – in the car he had just come from! Unlike racing teams, the rally mechanics had followed their usual practice and loaded the car with spares. The misunderstanding would cost them dear. Duggie Watts rushed back with him to fit it and Paul steamed off again, but by then the ailing Ravetto/Starrabba GTO had moved past into the class lead.

The Healey team, in a far from youthful car, had come within a smidgen of seriously embarrassing Ferrari in their own back yard, and it was a bitter pill to swallow. They had taken second in class and 20th overall, but this would be one occasion when the journalists preferred not to quote Paul. Henry Manney, of *Road & Track*, succinctly summed up Paul's feelings stating: 'Hawkins powered off in clouds of the Great Australian Adjective.' Enough said. There were times when journalism just wasn't worth it.

Following his success with Healey, both at Sebring and in so nearly taking their class in the Targa, he was next asked to team up with John Rhodes in ENX 415C, one of the two lightweight Sprites which had been specially wind-tunnel developed for Le Mans. These spaceframed, alloy-bodied flyers bore little resemblance to the road car of the same name, and boasted a Laycock four-speed overdrive gearbox which, when mated to their screaming 1300cc engines and mere 660kg weight, meant they were capable of an impressive 148mph along the Mulsanne straight.

Paul was his usual forthright self, as John Rhodes remembers: 'The wonderful Australian accent, and the derogatory remarks about us Poms (he never changed), so the air was blue at Le Mans when he demanded a Panhard rod to locate the back axle to cure the weaving when the GT40 Fords overtook us at 200mph-plus. He also wanted a smaller steering wheel, but Geoff Healey would not hear of altering his car.

'Geoff also felt it was necessary for his cars to be seen, as the speed difference between the classes was considerable, so one was painted red and the other green in bright Dayglo paint. But the French disagreed, saying that it distracted other drivers. We had to repaint them with cheap vacuum-spray paint in a chicken shed behind the hotel. It wasn't very elegant...runs everywhere.

'At the start, cars were lined up facing the track, the drivers standing in a white circle opposite. The silence of the spectators before the flag dropped I shall never forget. It dropped and I ran over to the car. Would it start and away?'

Fortunately it did, and they were off on their respective stints, two hours on, two hours off, for the next 24. It was an era when teams were able to change drivers between cars, so when Paul found himself in difficulty from something he had eaten, and rushed into the pits to get it out of his system, Geoff was left to cover the offending results with a spade. Naturally enough, Paul was off-colour and not up to the pace, so Geoff substituted Clive Baker from sister car ENX 416C to rest him.

Unfortunately, Paul's 'little accident' had left Clive with a rather unpleasant situation, and as there was little in the way of ventilation to be had in the suffocating enclosure of the coupe, it seems likely indeed that he was longing for some air freshener. However, they drove on into the night, and John Rhodes recalls an earlier conversation: 'Paul understood the energy required for a 24-hour race, and foreign to me, eager to enjoy myself, had insisted on us not going out prior to the race, but resting for 24 hours. As dawn arrived the sun made it impossible to look through the windscreen; one had to check the position through the side window. Both Paul and myself had mechanical experience and didn't over-rev the engine. The only panic I had was an occasion when the engine suddenly did over-rev – the gearbox oil was aerating, causing the overdrive to slip. Into the pits, and some fresh oil cured the problem.'

There remained two more crises as the race drew to its climax. At the final pit stop John jumped out of the car to report that the brakes had failed. Geoff Healey quickly asked Paul if he could drive a car with no brakes, and he promptly piled in and set off to complete the last stint, for the honour of the team; and the extra tenner Geoff had promised. Quite how he managed at the end of the Mulsanne for the next two and a half hours might have been interesting to observe! Fate then decreed another hiccup. The Baker/Aaltonen car, then running eighth, suddenly retired with a blown engine, just two hours before the end, leaving 415C to uphold the honours, winning the 1300cc class and taking 12th place overall; they also won third prize in the Index of Thermal Efficiency and left, as John says, 'feeling very proud'. In a footnote to events, the cars would later be fitted with a Panhard rod, and a smaller steering wheel.

By the end of the endurance racing season, Paul had accrued not only class wins at both Sebring and Le Mans, but seconds at Marlboro, Maryland (in a Lotus Cortina shared with Roy Pierpoint) and Sicily, and a sixth at Reims in Mike de Udy's Porsche 904. This was better than a 60 per cent hit rate from just six sports car and saloon events – very different indeed to his comparatively poor Formula One and Two experiences, where his South African win stood alongside an Alexis success at Nürburgring as the only two podium places. Unsurprisingly he would shift focus away from open-wheelers to the faster and more powerful sports cars he so enjoyed, a decision additionally influenced by that earlier mentioned chance meeting.

'It was at the Nürburgring', says Jackie Epstein. 'They used to run a Formula Two race on what they called the short circuit; the Eifelrennen. I was having trouble in practice with the gearbox, and there was something wrong with it. It kept making a filthy howling noise and I knew something would break. Whilst I was scratching around the paddock with the gearbox in bits all over the floor, this brash Aussie appeared, whom I didn't know from a bar of soap. He sort of had a look and said: "Matey...you've got a problem." I said: "Yes, I have", and explained what it was. Paul sat down and said: "We'll have a look at it", and of course we got covered in oil and filth and fixed it.

'He was driving an Alexis, a not very successful Formula Two car, but he won the race. (It would be Alexis' only win in three seasons of the 1000cc F2 regulations.) Anyhow, we got talking...I did a few Formula Two races around Europe, not very successfully, and then he rang me up one day and said: "How would you like to go to South Africa for the winter?" This sounded like an excellent idea, and when Paul added: "If you can get a decent sports car, I can get you a decent deal to do the Nine-Hours and the subsequent five races," it was all systems go for the Springbok series.'

Jackie continues: 'I'd been hankering after a sports car anyway. They're big and strong, and for me, as I was then quite heavy, it was a much more practical proposition. We sat and talked about it in London, and I said: "If you sew up the deal with the South Africans, I'll get the car and we'll do the series." In those days the South African Motor Racing Club was run by Alex Blignaut, who was quite a good operator. He set us up a good deal. The nub of it was that we could go out there and, provided we started all the races, we could see ourselves through the whole three months at no cost to ourselves. Whether we won any *money* would be a different matter, and in those days start money was important.'

It quickly transpired that there were actually only two suitable cars available. One was the GT40, the other was a Ferrari LM. Col Ronnie Hoare, who was boss of English & Co, of Bournemouth – forerunners of Maranello Concessionaires – were the Ferrari importers for the UK. 'The colonel' had an LM which had done about 100 miles on the road, never been raced, and was in road trim. Meanwhile, John Wyer had one GT40, but the GT40 at that time was a very unknown quantity. It was a brand new car, very untested, and had been having a lot of trouble with the engine. 'We talked all this through, and of course David Piper had a long history of success out there (in South Africa) with Ferraris of various kinds, including an LM, and I said to Paul that we would go for the LM because it was a known quantity. He said "OK". He didn't mind, and it was up to me. So I bought the LM, drove it back from Bournemouth to West Kingsdown, and we turned it from a road car into a racer. We did quite a lot of work to it, threw a lot of it away, and it got quicker and quicker. And so we went out to do the Nine-Hours.'

It was to prove an encouraging debut for the new partnership, despite a spot of bother early on. Jackie: 'We lost a lot of time just after the start. It was the first race we'd done with the car, and we'd done very little testing. Paul took the start and after two or three laps I could hear it was down a cylinder, and it took me a bit of a time to get him to come in. When he did come in I said it was out on one cylinder, but he said: "No, no, it's going fine." We felt all the exhaust pipes, and sure enough one of them was stone cold.

'The trouble was that the engine in the LM was all packed in behind panels – you couldn't get at it. By the time we'd got the panels off and changed the plug – it was a pig of a job – we'd actually lost 10 minutes. But we'd already agreed it was bullet-proof, so we drove the thing flat-out, and hoped that the Sutcliffe/Ireland GT40, running second, would break. It didn't, but we came third overall behind the winning 365 P2 of Piper and Attwood. And that's what started my relationship with Paul.'

Chapter Six

Surfin' USA

It was to be a relationship that would last over three years, crossing three continents as the pair charged their way around the world. Jackie Epstein: 'Paul liked me driving with him because we had an agreement between us. He would go round the factories first because obviously they could pay serious money. He would see what they were going to pay, and whether the car was competitive. The one thing about Paul was that the competitiveness of the car was the primary issue. If he felt his chances were better with Ferrari, or Ford, or Porsche, that was fine. If he didn't, then we'd team up again. The seat was always open until two or three weeks before the race.

'Several times he came and drove with me rather than take a factory offer. We would always hand the car over as we found it. Brake pedal where it was, temperature gauge where it was, max RPM indicator where it was. That was our dogma between us. We'd work a strategy, and by and large that worked. Whereas most people used to change around every two hours, we didn't. We always used to do two stints apiece. We found we were both quicker in the second stint when we'd settled in. He would be the guy to win it, so long as I gave it him back every four hours.'

As usual, Paul would thoroughly enjoy his winter in South Africa. He drove David Good's Lola T70 to good effect with a first at Kyalami and a second in Rhodesia. He would also pilot Tim Parnell's modified Lotus 25 and, with the dawn of the new

Formula One 3-litre regulations on the horizon, and a four-pot 2.7-litre Climax banging away behind, he managed a pair of third placings against team-mate Innes Ireland, in his similar BRM V8-engined car – and a certain Jack Brabham, who was giving his Repco Brabham its debut at the East London circuit prior to formalizing his place in the history books.

Jackie, meanwhile, was as good as his word, and as Paul chopped and changed between three cars, he took his Ferrari LM to a well-earned third at the James McNiellie circuit in Rhodesia, following it up with a fourth at Kyalami, and a speeding ticket for clocking 112.5mph in a 35 zone.

'Paul had a deal (what a surprise!) that we could go out to the Kruger game reserve for three or four days,' says Jackie, 'just watch the animals and get pissed. There were four of us in the car. There was no hurry, it was a lovely day and we were wandering along up to Kruger. We were going along quite happily near Springs, just outside Jo'burg, at about 60mph, and I saw this bloke standing in the road waving his hat. I was going to take no notice, but Paul said: "Matey, I think you'd better stop." So I did, and this guy comes pounding down the road and sticks his head in the window. He's got a stopwatch. So he stops the watch, looks at it, pulls out these charts and goes all the way down to the very last thing on it, and says: "Yussus, man, that is quick!" I looked at the man in amazement; I hadn't any idea what he was talking about. So then another guy comes pounding down the road, and it turns out they were running a speed trap.'

Needless to say, the saga of the speeding ticket was comparatively big news at the time, and soon ended up not only in the newspapers, but in court, where Jackie took the brave step of calling on expert witnesses, amongst whom was a certain Australian racing driver with something of a reputation for bending the rules of the road. Perhaps unsurprisingly, it would take 12 months to settle the action, of which Jackie would eventually be acquitted, but at least he wasn't the unwitting recipient of one of Paul's tirades on the dangerous driving practices of the police.

February was the next outing of the 'International' car, as the Ferrari was now known. Jackie: 'We'd brought it back to England, and after a quick rebuild on the engine, because it had worn out its piston rings in South Africa, we shipped it to the States with its trailer in a hurry, got ourselves a hire car, bought a tow ball and shot off down to Daytona.'

While their race would end with gearbox problems after a brave 425 laps, it would be the trip down to the circuit that would indelibly influence not only Paul's future, but the serenity of many of his friends as he and Jackie discovered the source of a small yet alarmingly explosive device, originally designed as a trucker's fog warning. He would never again have to make another acetylene bomb.

'We were going down to Daytona with the LM and there were these little roadside huts all the way from New York down to Daytona (about 600 miles on the coast road). Little huts that sell pecan nuts. But they also sell M80s, as these things are called. They had a 10-second fuse, and we also discovered that they would go off underwater. So we stocked up on hundreds of these things. Anyway, we were in the hotel at Daytona after practice, and we had a room high up near the top – sixth floor – and Paul says: "Matey...a bit of sport here." So he lights one and flushes it down the loo!

'Next thing, there's a howling of police sirens and Christ knows what else, and we look out the window and there's four cop cars outside, flashing blue lights; the whole bittsie. What's happened is it's gone down two or three floors and gone off under some poor old biddie sitting on the loo! And of course all hell broke loose, so we got undressed, got into bed and pretended we were asleep. Of course, the hotel management knew it had to come from somewhere, but they never did find out (until now!). From this time forward, Paul would become the scourge of his friends, often assisting constipation difficulties by rolling them into toilet cubicles.

Just a few weeks later, and the hubbub of Sebring brought

Deluge in Daytona – another of Paul's M80s finds the spot.

Paul back to the USA, paired once again with the accomplished rally exponent Timo Makinen, with whom he would take the Donald Healey Sprite to a class win and an impressive 18th overall against some pretty heavyweight machinery. In fact, included in the 17 cars in front of them were no less than five Ford GTs , five Porsches and two Cobras. Not a bad record for a car sporting a mere 1300cc.

Clearly Paul was still capable of making the best of his small-car experience with John Sprinzel, while Frank Gardner's story shows he still retained his sense of fun – particularly now that he had M80s and had discovered that these things worked under water. Frank: 'While we were having a meal in New England he dispensed one off in a swimming pool which was of aluminium construction. By the time the evening meal was finished, so was the swimming pool. The evidence was an empty pool and a very wet car park; with the hotel personnel irate, and Paul impressed with his achievement.'

As the Sebring race was a major event on the sports car calendar, teams and drivers had congregated from all over the world, bringing with them their personal and cultural preferences. Naturally, amongst Paul's contributions would be his extensive vocabulary, including numerous variations of 'bloody', his beer drinking ability, and his water skiing experience. 'Paul taught Paddy Hopkirk (of Monte Carlo Mini fame) to water-ski at one stage,' continues Frank. 'Paul gave the original demonstration, as he was a competent water skier, then Paddy was readied for the fray. Paul prepared his skis by removing the keels, and to use a pair of skis without keels required considerable skill. Paul then sat on the bank offering advice to Paddy, and after about 300 falls Paddy was thoroughly waterlogged and decided that water-skiing wasn't for him. We all called it a day and went home, and I am never sure if Paddy worked it out.'

It seems, however, that Paddy nevertheless enjoyed himself on this occasion, as he was later reported as having a great time water-skiing on the lake near Avon Park with Paul and others, including Graham Hill and Jackie Stewart, whose Alan Mann GT40 would not last the distance at Sebring. Just a few days later that same car would be used for Le Mans testing, not only by Hill and Stewart, but also by Paul, blissfully unaware of the importance it would have in his later life.

As spring slowly turned to summer, contacts initiated with Tim Parnell in South Africa metamorphosed into a handful of drives in Britain and Europe, though none provided the elusive podium places he so earnestly sought, and by the time Le Mans came around in mid-June his days of driving open-wheelers were almost done. Others might have expressed regret at the lost opportunity, but ever the optimist, 'laughing boy' Paul would never be heard bemoaning what might have been. It would be the future that beckoned him.

Now, as Epstein's 'International' car saw Paul's name more frequently associated with big-capacity sports cars, manufacturer teams began to take notice of the experienced privateer, and first to confirm serious metal would be the old retainer from his Willment days – Ford.

It is now well-known history that Ford were intent on taking Le Mans away from Ferrari, and that is a story in itself, but the effort, expense and engineering might that was utilized to do so almost beggars belief. No less than 13 Ford GTs, including eight of the loping 7-litre Mk 2s, were lined up against 14 of the Italian prancing horses in 1966. The 427 cubic inch monsters were capable of hitting over 200mph and the Ford sledgehammer would include a trio of Holman and Moody Mk 2s driven by Andretti/Bianchi, Bucknum/Hutcherson and Hawkins/Donohue. However, team-mate and co-driver Mark Donohue was apparently feeling somewhat slighted that the 'experienced' Hawkins should be named as senior driver of the two, particularly as from his point of view, his co-driver had only driven Le Mans before in dinky little Sprites.

It wasn't long before a drama in practice saw the rear bodywork of Paul's car launched into orbit as the car hit full whack along the Mulsanne straight. As usual, he was up to the job, and somehow managed to keep the spinning, howling machine glued to the ground, to the praise of Henry Ford II (who *just happened* to be in France for the weekend to observe his company's third attempt to humble Ferrari!).

Henry seemed to think that the boy had done well, reputedly backing up his view with some welcome hard cash, though it is just more than possible that he was also thinking of the close PR disaster Ford had just avoided, for April testing had seen the unfortunate death of Walt Hansgen whilst driving a Ford GT40. They could do without similar adverse publicity on the very weekend that had been so long planned as the pinnacle of the company's achievement, and it was Paul's skill at the wheel that had just saved them from potentially huge embarrassment.

At that time Peter Jackson was also in the pits, being shown around by Paul, who would always remember his friends from the past, no matter how great his fame in future years. 'He was completely unfazed by the enormous moment,' says Peter. Perhaps, too, Paul's face-saving antics on the Mulsanne also impressed his new co-driver Donohue, as later in the year Mark would welcome him into his house.

Race day dawned to a line-up of 55 cars covering no less than 11 marques, and the bronze-coloured number 4 Hawkins/Donohue car was off to a reasonable start. But it wouldn't last. Within an hour they had pitted with a broken drive-shaft, taking a further hour to replace it, and by then the damage had been done. Even before the misty sun sank below the stands they were out of the running with a broken differential.

Rouen in July would be Paul's final fling in the Parnell Formula Two Lola, and after a 12th lap puncture his open-wheeler days were now over. His indomitable spirit, though, was as ever flying high, and he soon arranged a deal with race commentator John Bolster and ERA punter Bill Morris, the latter having good reason to remember that final event. 'The first time I met Paul was at Rouen in 1966, where John Bolster was doing the commentary. At the end of the meeting John came up to me and said: "Would you like to come to Paris with Paul and myself?" Oh God! I was a 19-year-old and Paul was well into his thirties by then (in fact he was not quite 29), and John Bolster must have been 55 or something, so I said: "Of course, I'd love to, but I'm due back in England with my lot," because I was racing my ERA. So I went and saw them and asked if they could take the car back, and they said: "Yes, yes, of course we'll do that, you go and enjoy yourself."

'So I was bundled in the back seat of Paul's Ferrari (don't ask again), and John Bolster and Paul went in the front, and off we went to Paris. We had a very good meal, and then we went to a night-club, and we sat at the front and made a *heck* of a noise; or rather the other two made a heck of a noise and all I wanted was for the floor to open up and swallow me. The other two were shouting ribald comments to all the pretty ladies and everything else that came on stage, and eventually the *maître d'* got very upset and got on the stage and said there was apparently two English people at the front making a lot of noise, so he said: "Perhaps one of them would like to come up and take part in the next act?"

'Paul Hawkins was up on the stage *like that*. Well, the *maître d'* said: "To take part in the next act you have to allow this young lady here, when the music stops, to take one item of clothing off you, and you can take one off her." And within about five seconds flat they were both stark bollock naked on the stage, whereupon Paul picked this unfortunate girl up, jumped off the stage, roared through the watching audience and disappeared out the door.

'John Bolster said to me: "He'll be back shortly." Well, one o'clock came, two o'clock came, three o'clock came, four o'clock came, and no sign of Paul. We walked outside to see where we had left the Ferrari, and there was no sign of it, so John said: "I think we'll have to go back to England on the train." So we got on the train and went back to England. I didn't see Paul for another month. When he turned up I said: "Where did you get to?" and he said: "Oh, I went down to the South of France for a nice holiday," and that was the end of it.'

Perhaps he now finally saw that he would not make it in the world of Formula cars, or somehow recognized that it was a point of change, and from this time forward he would work toward becoming a top sports car driver. It was something he already had a talent for, if only he had looked at the past where his record already stood as testament to his ability. Perhaps there was a tinge of regret, but those who knew him never saw it evidenced, and a holiday was just what he needed right now. Whether the naked French *fille* joined him on his impulsive break we will never know – but we can guess. It was the beginning of a new era in his career.

Later that month it was announced that the 'International' car had been brought up to '66 specification and, fitted with its new Drogo nose, the 250/275 LM was headed to Australia for the Rothmans 12-Hours at Queensland's Surfers Paradise. It would be the first time that such an event would be held at the new circuit, sited to draw its crowds from both the Gold Coast holiday resort and the nearby State Capital of Brisbane. It would also be the first time that Paul had returned to Australia since stepping aboard the *Fairsea* nearly six years earlier.

He faced the trip with trepidation. It seems that whilst he had maintained limited contact with his brother John and sister Ruth, he had not been in touch with his father, and the last they had seen of each other was way back in '59, when they'd briefly met in Melbourne. As far as he was aware, his father's negative views on his motor racing career had not changed. 'He was very reluctant to go for several reasons,' says Jackie. 'The real root cause was that he didn't want to meet his dad.' But they went, and the Rothmans 12-Hours would be every challenge they had anticipated.

The first problem was one of pit crew, though brother John offered help, and as the grid slowly assembled it soon became clear that most of the eclectic local machinery would pose little challenge. A Cooper S-powered Mini Moke and a mixture of

89

saloons were not even in the same class, though there was serious competition to be had in the form of David McKay's *Scuderia Veloce* Ferrari 250 LM driven by Stewart/Buchannan, and the Sutcliffe/Matich GT40, not to mention a Porsche spyder and an Alfa TZ, which were both capable of quick times.

The Le Mans-type start saw Paul off in comfortable style. At first all was going as strategy dictated, and with a five-lap lead, he even found a bit of time to play cat and mouse with Jackie Stewart as they swapped positions, to the crowd's obvious approval, before steadily but firmly pulling away to further extend his lead. After the usual planned four-hour stint, he pitted for fuel and to hand over to Jackie.

The Ferraris were lapping quite a bit faster than the GT40, but a pit stop of over five and a half minutes gave three laps back to the Sutcliffe/Matich car, whose own stop was a salutary lesson in team efficiency. With four pit stops planned, the number 4 Epstein/Hawkins car would need to both minimize time in the pits, and fly like a bird on the two-mile circuit. Slowly at first, their 250 LM began using oil. It would not be a problem provided they stopped often enough to top up, though it would incur more otherwise unnecessary and ill afforded pit stop time.

Then it started to get into the alternator and stopped charging the battery. They were now losing time to both the GT40 and the Stewart/Buchannan car as the battery was replaced, and a temporary fix applied to the alternator in the form of a quick blast of fire extinguisher to neutralize the oil-covered component. Again on track, all seemed to be holding up reasonably until nightfall, when yet again the poorly fed battery needed replacement.

Oil by now had drowned the area surrounding the alternator, coating the fan belt and causing slippage. It had to be replaced, and although by now a win looked unlikely, they needed to stay in the race as the Matich GT40 and Stewart 250 LM fought for position. To change the belt, however, necessitated removal of the driver's seat, a complex job that would cost further expensive time. As the Stewart/Buchannan car howled around the circuit in its bid to cut the gap to the Sutcliffe/Matich Ford, the crowd thoroughly enjoying the spectacle, the author, who was watching from trackside, would be forever smitten by the sounds, smells and spectacle of endurance sports cars. Jackie and Paul regained the circuit to be classified third in class, and the GT40 was acclaimed winner across the line. However, it would later be successfully appealed by the entrant of the Stewart/Buchannan car, whose last-hour charge had proved successful. And Paul would finally meet with his father, on the very day they left to return to England, discovering to his delight that he was now his number-one fan.

At the end of August, and back in the UK, it was announced that Paul would be driving a Mercury Cougar in the British Saloon Car Championship, but it would never happen. While he had never been very keen on saloons, it was now obvious to him that he needed his own wheels if he was to capitalize on his steadily progressing career, but his 'matey', Jackie Epstein, was also looking for change.

An opportunity had arisen in the shape of a series in the US, which promised big money when compared to the ever-shrinking purses in the UK. 'We'd considered the idea of doing the CanAm,' says Jackie. 'We both wanted to do it. I went to Eric Broadley and said: "Look, I want to do the CanAm as a privateer (he was already backing Surtees as a factory car) and there's certain things we want done with this car a bit differently." He agreed he'd build the car the way we wanted it.'

On August 26 a spanking new Lola T70 Mk 2 was delivered to his workshops. Paul, meanwhile, was into raising cash for his new project, and as a wheeler-dealer of some standing was in the business of selling the occasional car. It was not the first time that he had raised cash in this way, as John Sprinzel recalls of his days at Lancaster Mews: 'I know he rebuilt a wrecked Sprite out of bits and pieces in the workshop, and sold it to race car driver Ian Burgess. I didn't discover the 'mystery' Sprite that Ian bought until after Paul had left, so I didn't ever tax him with it…he did enough for me to deserve a little extra earner'.

By now Paul had gone upmarket and found a D-Type Jag on his last trip in South Africa. After some fettling it was up for sale with an asking tag of £2500. With its twin headrests and Le Mans history its sale was soon assured, and he now had a few more pounds burning a hole in his pocket for the Championship tin-top he fancied in the States.

The bright orange Lola CanAm car was now ready for action, and with its Alan Smith-built 6-litre V8 giving 450bhp of grunt, it was rolled out for its inaugural run within days of its delivery. Jackie: 'In fact we'd made a slight mistake. From our sports car days we thought we'd better give the transmission an easier time as gearboxes used to break more than the engines, so we had Lola build a car with doughnuts in the transmission, which Eric Broadley had never done before.

'We thought we'd better have one race in England before we went to America, and we did Brands Hatch with it, and we realized in the middle of that meeting that we'd made a mistake. We'd used the largest doughnuts we could find, but what we didn't realize was that the doughnuts stored energy. In the big GT cars it didn't matter, but in a lightweight CanAm car, when you came off the throttle and the doughnut was wound up, it kept going. Not much, but enough to upset your line into the corner. It was only about 10 days before we had to ship the car to America, so we had a council of war and had it swapped back to standard, then went out and did the CanAm with it.'

They would stay with Mark Donohue (his Le Mans co-driver) whilst in the north-east of the country, as Jackie recalls: 'St Jovite lives in my memory. It's a little known track (in Canada, north of Montreal), although it's now being revived and rebuilt. We started practising, and St Jovite in those days was unique in as much as it had a hill in the main straight – a very *pointed* hill in quite a *long* main straight. Now one of the regulation changes was that they'd altered the rules for CanAm, and you didn't have to carry a spare wheel anymore, so they just took the spare wheel out, modified the front a bit, and it was that much lighter. So we went to St Jovite with a brand new car gloriously untested, with this hill, and in the second day's practice there was this howling gale blowing the wrong way up this hill.'

It was to prove a disastrous combination of wind, crest, lightened car and a flat-chat speed of nearly 170mph. As the Lola crested, catching dollops of air under its front spoiler, the undertray took on sail-like proportions, launching it like a fighter plane into the stratosphere. It took off in a blow-over of horrendous proportions, flipping in mid-air and crashing upside-down on top of Paul.

Jackie: 'The thing just turned over on its back...flat out. As Paul said, he could feel his hat grinding away, so he kept turning his head and when it finally stopped and they turned the thing back on its feet, he was all right except that his crash helmet had three dirty great grooves worn across it. He was all right (apart from a few bruises), but the car was pretty sad. Mechanically it was pretty sound – it hadn't bent the chassis or anything like that – but the body was scrap.

'We hung around for the final day's practice, and Hugh Dibley, another Lola privateer, appeared and we said: "Look, Hugh, for Christ's sake, if the wind's blowing back right off or throw some lead into the front of the car or do something. "Yes, yes, yes", he said, "I hear what you're saying." Anyway, he had exactly the same problem except that because we'd warned him he had done something to the car as it didn't turn on its back. His just flew in the air like an aeroplane for about 100 or 150 yards the right way up. And it landed on a tree stump that cut the car clean in half. Again, it didn't hurt him. They were both lucky.

'In those days the Lola agent in America was Carl Haas, and they rushed around and flew us out a new body. We did a hasty rebuild on the car and went on to the next race. In fact we never got around to painting it. It did the rest of the CanAm in primer.' Paul's trusty helmet was naturally the worse for wear, and his usual British Racing Green with gold stripe and kangaroo-fronted mantle would thereafter change to all gold.

The series, however, did not light the fuse of fame for Paul, even if there were still plenty of M80s going off, and by the time they reached California for the finale of the series at Las Vegas, he had accumulated only two points from a fifth place at Mosport, and a podium third at the non-series North West GP at Pacific Raceway.

The trip across to Vegas was also memorable. Jackie: 'We got into Edwards Air Force Base by mistake, and Paul, of course, gets out and starts taking pictures of rockets. I mean, we shouldn't have been in there anyway, and eventually there's a howling of sirens and we were escorted out.'

While it would be the works Lola of John Surtees that took the series win, Paul as usual refused to be downhearted, as Jackie recalls: 'The last race was at Las Vegas, and they had a prize-giving that night in a hotel, and the room where it took place was on the first floor, with big open panoramic windows. We were all having a bit of a laugh and stirring it up, so we went to the supermarket and bought a jumbo-sized box of washing powder, and before we went in – all reasonably smart – to go up to this prize-giving, we dumped the entire contents of this washing powder in the big fountain outside. The water spray went nearly up to the first-floor windows. So we had the prize-giving as always – big table, being dished out – and the organizers had their backs to the window. We were all stood there, all very solemn and clapping politely, and this fountain was erupting. It was getting higher and higher past these windows, and of course eventually the whole place burst out in fits of laughter, and of course the organizers couldn't see it.' 'Hawkeye' had struck again!

Chapter Seven

The big rock candy mountain

While the CanAm might not have been the pinnacle of Paul Hawkins' career, it was just a few months later, on May 14th, 1967, when the world really took notice of him. Paired with Rolf Stommelen in a factory-entered Porsche 910/8, they walked away with one of the world's greatest sports car events – the Targa Florio.

The Targa had been inaugurated back in 1906, and one of the oldest races in the world would have a profound impact on the now 29-year-old 'Hawkeye'. In winning this race he could no longer be dismissed as just another journeyman, for to win in Sicily was as important at that time as Le Mans or Nürburgring. Perceptions would change, and the Targa would seal his career not only as a potent competitor, but as a winner of top-class international events.

The saga really starts, however, with Vic Elford, who was about to drive his first ever Targa with Porsche and who, of course, had bumped into Paul, his old rally oppo from their days with Sprinzel. 'We all went to Stuttgart and were driving down in a whole convoy of cars – engineers, drivers, mechanics. We had probably ten or a dozen cars, all of which were going to be used as recce cars for the Targa. Paul and I shared a car, and we were tail-end Charlie all the way down through Italy.

'All went well until we got to Naples, and we had no idea where we were going. At some point we were going across some *massive* intersection, and everybody made it except us, and we got some little old guy on a Vespa scooter stuck across in front of us. I was driving and I started hooting and trying to get him out of the way, and Paul says: "Don't worry, mate, I'll move the f***ing bastard". In those days he and the other Australians (and a lot of other drivers, too) used to carry around a bunch of little firebombs, so Paul reaches around into the back of the car into his bag and pulls out one of these little round fireballs, lights it...opens the door and just rolls it under the guy's Vespa...and all hell was let loose.' It might have been mayhem, but they made it to the ferry.

While Paul introduced Vic to the grappa bars of Sicily, Porsche team manager Huschke von Hanstein had every intention of winning the race, a round of the 1967 International Championship for Makes. Although a non-factory Porsche had won in '66, opposition remained strong, and on partisan Sicilian soil, the might of Ferrari and Alfa Romeo could never be taken lightly.

A quartet of V8 Alfa Romeo 33s making their European debut were a considerable threat; earlier that year they had shown themselves to be a good half-second a lap faster than the Porsches at Sebring. Previous winner Vaccarella was also back, along with team-mate Scarfiotti in a P4 Ferrari, supported by the P3 of Müller/Guichet, while Phil Hill and Hap Sharp piloted the innovative Chaparral 2E. Against these and other opposition, von Hanstein entered a steamroller of no less than six of Porsche's nimble 910s. Three sported the usual 2-litre flat-sixes whilst a second trio were fitted with 2195cc, 272bhp eight-cylinder engines and all were well suited to the mountainous terrain.

The experienced 'Hawkeye', who had driven the race on two previous occasions, was teamed with up and coming Cologne rally ace Rolf Stommelen in one of the larger-engined cars, which would run with its roof panel removed to accommodate Stommelen's height. They were strenuously instructed by Huschke to set a relaxed easy pace. No matter what, theirs was

Paul's first car was a Holden, but he replaced it with this MG TC to give himself more street cred and raceability.

Soon the TC would give way to an Austin-Healey BN2, but it was this 100S owned by friend Terry Valmorbida which for the first time put serious power under Paul's right foot.

A 'demo drive' with owner Valmorbida beside him soon led to an offer of some race drives; here's Paul leading a Sprite and another 100S at Melbourne's Albert Park.

By 1960 he was racing in England, thanks to John Sprinzel. Here he is in Sprite S221 chasing an Elva Courier in the Tourist Trophy race at Goodwood.

No problem for Paul renewing his Australian competition licence, but a UK driver's licence was declined after he had terrified the examiner!

Never too proud to learn, in 1961 Paul took himself off to Cooper's racing drivers school at Brands Hatch for an assessment; it would appear that they were duly impressed!

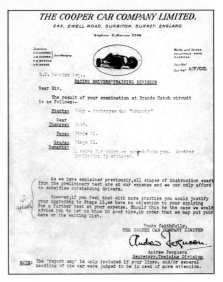

1962 saw Paul graduate to a fully professional racing team with Ian Walker, seen here alongside Paul in the Lotus 23 with which class wins and fastest laps would come aplenty.

Driving for Walker meant useful variety, for the team also ran Paul in a Formula Junior Lotus 22, seen here with chief mechanic John Pledger, ex-Team Lotus, in attendance.

For 1963 the Walker team switched to Brabham BT6s for the last season of Formula Junior racing; here's Paul heading for third place at Silverstone in one of them.

When the Willment team went racing in South Africa they took a Galaxie, a Lotus Cortina and a Cobra, all backed by Ford. This is Paul at Kyalami, his turn to drive the team's heavy metal.

Teamed with Timo Makinen, Paul's first race in the Targa Florio came close to scoring a class win in this Big Healey, complete with front bumper borrowed from a spectator's car.

Paul giving the Lotus 33 an airing at Silverstone in the 1965 International Trophy. Two weeks later he would give it a ducking in the harbour during the Monaco Grand Prix.

During the same busy month, Paul shared Mike de Udy's Porsche 904 in the Nürburgring 1000 Kms until a piston failed.

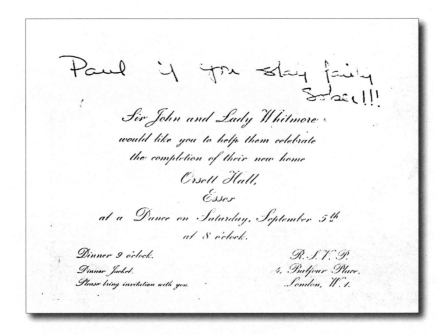

Paul 'f you stay fairly Sober!!!

Sir John and Lady Whitmore
would like you to help them celebrate
the completion of their new home

Orsett Hall,
Essex

at a Dance on Saturday, September 5ᵗʰ
at 8 o'clock.

Dinner 9 o'clock.
Dinner Jacket.
Please bring invitation with you.

R.S.V.P.
4, Balfour Place,
London. W.1.

Paul's partying antics were all too well known when Sir John Whitmore sent him this invitation to a house-warming with a cautionary message attached!

Paul giving Epstein's new Lola T70 a run in the 1966 Guards Trophy race at Brands Hatch prior to its CanAm season.

Jackie Epstein, whose driving partnership with Paul proved so fruitful for them both.

A change of car and country. Paul is back home after more than five years and about to begin the Rothmans 12 Hours in Epstein's Ferrari 250/275 LM.

Paul in his third Targa Florio, this time as a Porsche works driver and heading for victory in the 910/8 he shared with Rolf Stommelen in 1967.

In discussion with Porsche team manager Huschke von Hanstein, with whom he had a prickly relationship despite his successes with the team.

Another change of car. This is the factory-entered Ferrari 330 P4 which Paul shared with Jonathan Williams at Brands Hatch in the BOAC Six Hours. All was well until the dislodged rear bodywork flew off.

A memento from one of Paul's fun-filled 'winter' seasons in South Africa by the artist who previewed the race at Killarney.

Another big day. This time at Monza, where Paul and co-driver David Hobbs received the champagne for winning the 1968 1000 Kms race in the Gulf-sponsored Ford GT40.

Another one for the sideboard! Paul clutching the handsome trophy after the Monza race.

Talented team-mates. Gulf team chief John Wyer paired off Brian Redman with Jacky Ickx and David Hobbs with Paul for the 1968 endurance races at Brands Hatch, Monza and Spa, and the team's Ford GT40s were winners each time.

Paul shares a joke with Gulf Oil's Grady Davis while John Wyer, as always with pen and paper at the ready, enjoys the banter.

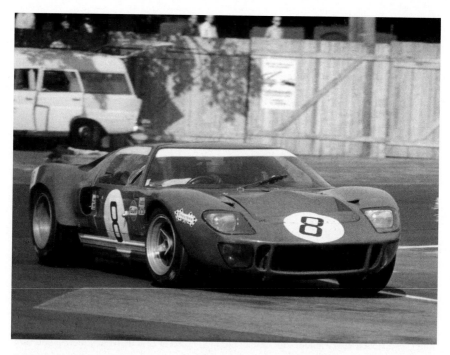

Paul's own GT40, AMGT2, had a busy 1968 season. A split water pipe would stop it here at the Norisring, but later he won at the Nürburgring before selling the car.

AMGT2 again, this time in the Guards Trophy race at Brands Hatch, where a puncture prevented him from winning the *Autosport* Championship for the second year running.

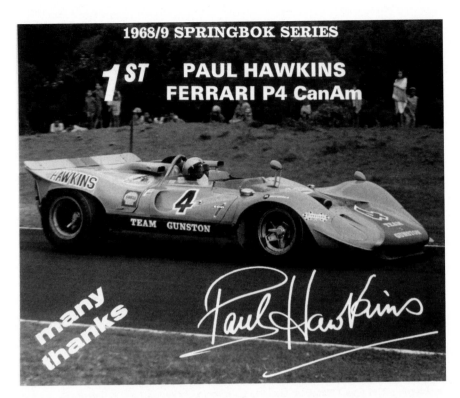

1968/9 SPRINGBOK SERIES

1ST PAUL HAWKINS
FERRARI P4 CanAm

many thanks

After his last trip to South Africa, Paul commissioned this 'thank you' picture which he gave to all who had helped him to win the Springbok series in the ex-David McKay Ferrari P4 which he raced with Gunston sponsorship.

This is just some of the silverware that came Paul's way during the course of his highly successful and varied racing career.

The award which meant as much to him as any; the impressive Shell Trophy awarded to the winner of the Springbok series.

Just testing. The Lola T70 Mk 3b about to be given a shakedown run in preparation for the 1969 season.

Paul Hawkins Racing Ltd had become the development arm of Lola and was now operating out of the factory premises.

The day before he died, Paul spent nearly two hours in this church at Little Budworth, near Oulton Park. Some said it was to shelter from the rain, but his father, a minister of religion, hoped it was rather more than that.

The end was to come on the circuit where Paul had had so many successes; the Lola being driven around Oulton Park for the last time.

'Hawkeye' as so many like to remember him. Full of fun and repartee.

to be the car that was going to finish the gruelling 10 laps of the difficult road circuit.

Far from wanting to play the tortoise role, 'Hawkeye' reckoned that to win the Targa you had to be a local boy like Vaccarella, who by now could draw every one of its 898 curves from memory, or you needed to have St Christopher himself sitting beside you reading out the pace notes, rally-style. Knowing Paul could hardly be called a religious man, perhaps the Saint himself decided to intervene that day; or was it simply sheer determination and skill? No matter. The resulting win was a pivotal career point, and life for Paul Hawkins would never be quite the same again. He would later tactfully describe his experience in *Autosport* magazine...*sans* verbal embellishment.

'I went down to Sicily a month before the Targa Florio to learn the circuit in a Porsche road car. I had raced a 250 LM Ferrari and an Austin-Healey 3000 there before but, with something like 890 corners on the 42-mile circuit, I was finding it quite difficult to relearn. Vic Elford was sharing the car with me, and as a rally driver he seemed to be able to remember the course extremely easily. I was shattered to find that he could sit in the hotel room and start describing long stretches of the road, with details of corners, cambers and surfaces!

'Team manager Huschke von Hanstein took note of all our lap times down there, and from these times he was able to work out driver pairings for the race. I was to drive with Rolf Stommelen, and I took him for a lap in unofficial practice to show him the way round. I'd done all my laps until then with no incidents at all, but on this one lap, with Rolf in the car, we had five or six narrow escapes – we nearly hit a truck, we nearly hit a car head-on, a donkey walked straight across the road in front of us, and we slid right across the road on one corner at 120 and nearly hit a tourist in a Porsche coming the other way! When we got back to the pits Rolf said to von Hanstein: "The bloke's mad – I don't ever want to go in a car with him again!"

'We were to race an eight-cylinder car and halfway through my first official lap of practice I was really motoring, leaping and jumping as the Porsche took off on bumps, but a drive-shaft broke. There was nothing I could do about it because I was about 20 miles from the pits, so I stripped off to my underpants and lay in the sun until Rolf came round to collect me in a six-cylinder car!

'Some stronger drive-shafts were flown out of Stuttgart, but for the first couple of laps [of the race] I took it easy, not trying to stay with Vaccarella in the works P4 Ferrari. Rolf did his three laps, and I set off on the final four, but found that I was losing concentration. I hadn't eaten anything all day and I didn't really feel hungry because it was so hot. I'd had an orange just before I took over again, and the noise in the cockpit together with the smell of hot oil was making me feel sick. All the mineral water I'd been drinking probably hadn't helped either, so I put my finger down my throat and made myself sick. After that I felt much better and I was able to concentrate for the final laps, since we were in the lead then anyway.

'When Vaccarella's Ferrari crashed, the spectators had suddenly cottoned on to the fact that THEIR car wasn't leading, and suddenly I was having to swerve around big rocks and stones that had been rolled into the middle of the road. On the last lap I came sailing into a village at about 120 to find the local village idiot standing in the middle of the road! I missed him by about a foot. The Porsche team were really pleased with our win, because Porsches had also taken second and third places.'

Paul had previously driven a 906 to fourth place at the 'Ring for Porsche, though his views of the organization had altered little since his experiences with Mike de Udy's 904 back in '64. It was easy to understand why. Mike's car had just been returned from a complete factory rebuild, though from the practice times they were getting you would hardly know it. Paul had concluded that the car wasn't tracking correctly, which, according to the Porsche mechanics was simply an impossibility. It had been rebuilt by Porsche. They were the experts. Their modern, up-to-date, high technology said so. It *must* be tracking correctly, so quite what they thought as Paul took to their settings with a ball of string, a few oil drums and a fair dollop of rustic know how will perhaps never be known, but his lap times were soon credited by many as faster than the factory cars; even if the official timer disdainfully disagreed. Entrenched attitudes such as these were anathema to Paul and his Aussie sense of 'fair play'. This was exactly the sort of organizational high-handedness that he loathed, and whilst Paul's *Autosport* story skims the surface, Jackie Epstein's presence at the Targa that year offers valuable first-hand insight.

Jackie had entered the 'International' Lola T70 in the race; Hugh Dibley co-driving with him this year, whereas just 12 months earlier it had been Paul who had shared the drive with him in the 250 LM Ferrari for a creditable finish after considerable tyre problems. This year, the Lola would not last the distance, though its entry created an opportunity for Jackie and Paul to get together.

'He had supper with us at our hotel nearly every night and he'd tell me all the things that were going on. They were horrendous. He hated Porsche. He didn't like Huschke, and he didn't like their engineering attitudes. You know, they used to say: "Ve haff designed it. It iss perfect." And of course it wasn't. He got on alright with the mechanics, in fact he made a point of getting on with the mechanics because he knew that was half the battle, but what he didn't like about Porsche was that they were entrenched in their ideas.

'I remember halfway through practice he came to me one night and he said: "They're going to break their drive-shafts. There is no way these piddley little things are going to stand up, because the car's leaping in the air everywhere and lands with a bang. If you land on throttle you are going to break it. I land off throttle, but of course it's unstable and I might lose it." He created a huge stink, and sure enough one of them (Paul, of course) broke his drive-shaft in practice in the mountains, so they were stuck there for half the day. They finally listened to him and flew in stronger drive-shafts overnight. As he said: "They must have realized the problem. They must have designed and built these things months ago, but they didn't send them to the Targa." Charter an airplane and send them overnight...that was Porsche's thinking.'

If Paul had proved his point over the drive-shafts, perhaps his next modification was perhaps a little easier to adopt, if less effective. Jackie continues: 'He was always rowing with them about cockpit cooling. There wasn't any. We used to do that with all our cars. Cold air on your face keeps you sharp.' Paul got them to agree, and his car wore scoops throughout the race, even if, according to his later description, the cockpit still stank of fumes. His worries, though, were still not over, saying to Jackie: 'They've teamed me with a total unknown. I don't know if the guy is any good or not!' Porsche were boosting Stommelen as a top name, and from Paul's point of view they were spending a lot of money. As Jackie would later say: 'You don't go to Porsche cheap'.

As the race itself was more akin to one gigantic 44-mile long rally stage, with all competitors running on staggered times, it was hardly surprising that crowd control could be a bit of a problem, and Paul's story of finding someone stood in the middle of the road is further explored by Jackie's previous Targa experiences. 'In the days when crowd control was non-existent, for the first two or three miles after the pits you just drove at them. I mean, you had to memorize whether the road went left or right, and just drove at 'em. The young lads' trick was to jump back at the last minute, though up in the mountains it was very much better. The very first Targa I did, which was with the Cooper Monaco, was totally strange to me. We quickly discovered that the Mafia had it organized. They were brilliant. They didn't have control of the pits area, or the first two or three miles, but beyond that the marshals on each corner, usually up on the hill with a bottle of wine, were Mafia men. Spectators wouldn't dare push their luck or they'd have been ventilated! Once you got away from the immediate pits area, you had no worries about spectators, or cattle, or anything like that.' It rather leaves us wondering whatever happened to Paul's village idiot.

Fortunately, Paul's inexperienced team-mate Rolf Stommelen was made from the right stuff, and his three laps to Paul's seven proved he had the right mental attitude toward winning. Vic Elford would also enjoy the podium that year, taking a well-earned third place. Meanwhile, Paul remained unconvinced by Porsche's organizational cock-sureness. 'He saw the post-race party, but then he came down to us, and we carried on all night,' concludes Jackie. He was also pretty pissed off, as Huschke had already pocketed the prize money.

'I drove for Porsche again in the Nürburgring 1000 Kilometres,' continues Paul's *Autosport* article, 'but I had a six-cylinder car there and it wasn't handling as well as I would have liked. Mitter's eight-cylinder car broke down and lost the lead on the last lap, and my co-driver Koch passed Buzzetta's other works Porsche to take the lead – for a while it looked as though I was going to have won the Targa and the 1000 Ks one after the other! – but Buzzetta got past again late in the lap and Koch finished just a tenth of a second behind him. I was going to drive for Porsche at Mugello, too, but we eventually decided against it, as there wouldn't have been sufficient time for the pre-race testing and practice that Porsche like to be able to carry out.'

Apart from which, he could do without the aggro. Paul had now decided there were other fish to be fried. His stint with Porsche had certainly been successful, with a major win, a second and a fourth in his three races for them, though his personality and style were somewhat opposed to the authoritarianism and rigid self-belief they encompassed. Now he was winning with his own car, and it was time to move on.

Chapter Eight

Sittin' on top of the world

It was almost mid-season by the time 'Hawkeye' returned to the UK, and by now his name was not only associated with his recent international success, but also with numerous other wins and places across Europe and the UK. His progress was being watched closely by other factory teams, though to appreciate the reasons for this dramatic and fortuitous change of circumstance, the story needs to roll back to the USA, where the CanAm series had just finished and Paul, armed with starting money dollars to support his car sales income, was looking for the next season's mount.

Jackie: 'I took Paul out to Rattlesnake Raceway, with the intention of possibly buying the winner of the American saloon car series. Dan Gurney had a factory-prepared Fairlane with which he had just won the American tin-top series. Our original thought was that we would get this thing, bring it back to England, and Paul would drive it in the British saloon car series. That was the original intention, but whilst we were wandering around his workshops, what should we discover but a brand new GT40 tub in aluminium. And of course we looked at this, and at the end of a few days' discussion and a few beers, we bought the GT40 tub and all the spares that he had.'

This was in fact AMGT2, the Alan Mann car that Paul had tested at Le Mans, and its lightweight alloy tub and bodywork was a full 120lb lighter than a standard GT40. Following testing at the Sarthe circuit, the car had been shipped to the States, and was now about to re-cross the water to blighty, where Paul and Jackie would set to work. With its aluminium body and prototype designation it would not be eligible for the Group 4 series that Paul had in mind, and it needed some modification, so after replacing its body with standard glassfibre, they set about the tub.

Jackie: 'Strictly speaking, you weren't supposed to use an ally tub, so to get out of that little problem we skinned it in 24-gauge tinplate, so when scrutineers were out with magnets it would all be steel. It was still 50 kilos lighter.' They were now almost ready to go motor racing, the pair arranging that Jackie would act as Paul's logistics organizer for the UK series while Paul would see to continental races.

The scene was now set for the *Autosport* Championship, though there was still the little matter of the racing advantage to be considered, as Jackie continues: 'Amongst all the bits and pieces we brought back from America were three or four brand new cross-bolted blocks. Ford had cast the 289 block with cross-bolted mains. Again, strictly speaking, that wasn't allowed, and if anybody had ever taken the sump off, we would have had a bomb.'

With additional support from Castrol and Firestone, the new car's first outing at Snetterton could not have been better as Paul pushed it not only to a new record fastest lap, but profited by an error on the part of Denny Hulme in another Ford to take a flying first. Three days later, at Silverstone, he was again out to nail Denny, who would go on to become Formula One World Champion that year, but on this occasion it was Paul's turn to over-egg the pudding, spinning from Maggotts all the way to Becketts before making up places to finish a well deserved second to the quick Kiwi.

April, again at Silverstone, saw yet another podium place, and the new Ford – soon to be painted red (like his original Healey) – was proving to be an exceptional flyer, though in the meantime he had been keeping his eye open for other good drives, as his *Autosport* article illustrates.

'I reckoned that a works Ford drive would be the best bet for the races at Daytona, Sebring and Le Mans, and that a factory Porsche would stand a good chance at races like the Targa Florio, the Nürburgring 1000 Kilometres and the Circuit of Mugello. At Daytona, Fords were crippled with gearbox breakages and I missed a drive, while for Sebring they had decided to concentrate on just two works cars instead of the usual six or seven, so I didn't get a drive there either.'

In the meantime, Jackie had also been busy, selling on the CanAm Lola to make way for a new 'International'. This too had its roots in America, as he explains: 'Whilst out there Paul and I had this little council of war, and decided that what we needed for the following season was the very best coupe we could acquire and do most of the World Championship series again. I was on the 'phone almost every week to Eric Broadley because I knew he was in the middle of designing the T70.

'Now we had learned a lot from our Ferrari days and we'd also learned quite a lot from the CanAm as well. The T70 was designed to take a 5-litre Chevvy. Now for the CanAm car I had two 6-litre Chevvys. They were Alan Smith motors, and Alan Smith in those days was the finest engine builder in the world in my opinion. I mean, he could build Chevvys they couldn't build in America. What we had planned was that Eric would build the chassis, but we would supply our own engines.

'I kept phoning up Eric and saying: "Look, we need cockpit cooling, we need this, we need that." All these things we had learned and thought about. We took delivery the week before Spa. It was brilliant. You could run any sized engine, there wasn't a capacity limit and we already had two Smith 6-litres.

'Surtees was again running the factory car with the Aston engine. The Aston was a highly complex four-cam V8, all super high-tech and all that, but it was a triumph of ambition over engineering...and of course he was the (Lola) factory team. We wanted Chevvys from day one.

'Eric produced two cars just in time for Spa – my car and one for Mike de Udy. Mike's had a stock standard 5-litre Traco, as produced by the factory, and ours had a 6-litre. In practice this was a flyer. I mean, it was massively quicker than the Aston. It was as quick as the factory GT40s and nearly as quick as the 4-litre Ferraris. Paul dropped into the car brilliantly.'

Paul in *Autosport*: 'I'd hoped to do the Monza 1000 Kilometres in Jackie Epstein's Lola Mk 3 GT with a 5.9-litre Chevvy engine, but the car wasn't ready in time, and my first race was eventually with this car in the 1000 Kilometres race at Spa. I didn't have much time for practice to get the car set up properly, but it certainly went well in the race. What a wonderful car to drive! It went exactly where you wanted it to, and you could slide it confidently at 140–150mph in the wet. It didn't seem to be affected by side winds or other things that affect most cars, like uneven road surfaces or bumps in the middle of corners. We finished fourth in the race, and were quite pleased with ourselves because this was one of the first Mk 3 Lolas to race.'

In fact it was the very first time that the new Lola coupe had been driven anywhere in anger, and a fourth place, in the wet, first time out of the box, was absolutely incredible. As Paul pushed the car to its limits, slipping and sliding sideways in one of the best drives of his life, there would be only three cars finish in front of their privateer challenge – a factory Ford Mirage driven by Ickx/Thompson, the factory Herrmann/Siffert Porsche 910 and the factory Bianchi/Attwood Ferrari P4. Having already demonstrated his skills for Porsche, it would be surprising indeed if Ferrari and Ford had not taken notice of the Aussie upstart.

June, of course, was Le Mans time, and again Ford offered a drive. Paul's description continues: 'It's hard to describe the Ford set-up because it's so gigantic and they spend so much money, but they produce the best cars that money could buy to do the job Ford require them to do. And that is to win Le Mans. They had taken over half a big Peugeot garage in Le Mans, fitting it out with their own coffee and Coca-Cola machines, and they had even flown their own drinking water over from America! They had a big semi-trailer done out as a mobile workshop and I'm sure they would have flown that over too if they could have found a big enough plane. They even had their own toilet paper specially brought over from the States. We were looked after like kings – the best hotels in Le Mans, special caterers at the circuit, and caravans for us to sleep in out there.

'I was paired with Ronnie Bucknum and he did the start in the 7-litre Mk 2. He got away to a great start and led the race for over an hour until a water pipe sprung a leak through a fracture and we had to stop to weld the leak. Then we had to do another two laps without water because we hadn't done the mandatory 25 laps before we could add oil or water. We rejoined the race in 44th place and pressed on hard all through the night so that by dawn on the Sunday we were up to fifth place. It looked as though we could do even better than that, but the engine swallowed a valve going down Mulsanne and that was the end of Le Mans for us. But Ford had done what they planned to do; they had spent a lot of money, but they must have reckoned that the Gurney/Foyt win was well worth it. It's a pity that they won't be back there again next year.

'The Mk 2 Ford was the ideal car for Le Mans. I'm not so sure that it would have been very good at the 'Ring, but at Le Mans it was fabulous. It was easy to drive, although the steering was a bit heavy. The four-speed box had a nice gearchange, and that powerful smooth V8 of near enough to 7 litres really thundered the car along – although it gulped fuel at a fair old rate. We could only run for an hour on the 42 gallons in the tank. The highest speeds we were getting were around 210–220mph down the Mulsanne straight, which is fairly quick on what is after all just a French main road. Roaring down between the trees you didn't really get a great impression of speed looking straight ahead – but if you looked sideways and saw the telephone poles going by in a blur, you knew you were marching on. The Ford was comfortable to drive and very quiet. The most noise you hear inside is when you lift off and the air is sucked past the butterflies which are starting to close on the two big carburettors. I don't reckon Le Mans is the best race in the world by any means, but there's something magical about it. I don't know what it is, but I know that it's always been one of my ambitions to win at Le Mans, and with Fords I had one of the best chances of realising that ambition.

'I did the 12-hour race at Reims with Jackie Epstein in the Mk 3 Lola-Chevvy, sorting the car out successfully in practice and qualifying fastest ahead of Surtees and Hulme in their Lolas. I took the start steady to look after the clutch since we had full tanks and it was a long race, but I picked up the lead halfway round that first lap, and after 11 laps I broke the outright lap record at about 147mph – and that was in the dark on full tanks. The car was good. Reims isn't all that interesting, but it's fairly demanding. You can't afford to relax at all in these big fast cars, because you daren't risk getting the car even a foot out of position – especially not through the long fast one after the pits that you take at around 180. After three and a half hours we had worked up a lead of nearly a lap on Surtees, who was having troubles with his car. He stopped at the pits, and a few minutes later I stopped as well. I couldn't see the pit signals and I'd been trying to work out the laps in my head as to when I would have to stop for fuel. As it turned out I came in three laps early, but the gearchange was starting to feel sloppy and I mentioned this to Jackie before he took over. We had a look at the transmission and found a crack in the bellhousing, and that was the end of that race.'

It was a time when the honours of outright top speed and fastest lap average were important, and Reims, with its undulating tarmac triangle, had frequently vied with Le Mans for the honour. Paul and Jackie may not have finished, but with an extra high gear enabling them to pull 6000rpm, they had raised the lap record to a now unbeatable 236km/h (nearly 147mph), and Jackie is adamant that the plaque commemorating the event now hanging in Reims town hall should have Paul's name where his appears.

It was also an issue that the *Commission Sportive Internationale* was looking at very closely, and shortly after Le Mans (and Ford's win with the 7-litre) they announced regulation changes that would have a lasting influence on sports car racing, and upon privateer challengers such as Paul's. The nub of it was that prototypes would in future be limited to 3 litres, while sports cars with a minimum production of 50 would be limited to 5 litres.

At a stroke, it meant that their Alan Smith 6-litre engines would become redundant, and in future the Lola would have to be homologated as a 5-litre sports car if it wasn't to compete against the extensively financed factory prototypes. The balance of winning power would lie with those manufacturers large enough to produce 50 cars, or those with the engineering cash to develop new 3-litre machines. Privateers like Paul were not amused; not only at the decision itself, but at the way in which it had been taken. His sense of fair play was outraged, and this – twinned with his ongoing dislike of 'self-righteous pompous-arsed authority' – insulted his sensibilities. He was soon writing again to *Autosport* magazine.

'As a motor racing driver who earns his living by entering and driving racing cars I feel, along with most other people in the same position, that it is about time we had a properly representative body controlling our business of motor racing. Just how the various people in the RAC come to be there seems to be surrounded by a certain amount of mystery, as none of the race drivers, entrants or organisers are ever consulted about appointments to this governing body. We therefore have no true representatives.

'That the RAC delegate can go to the CSI meeting and vote for the 3-litre limit for Group 6 cars on behalf of British owners, drivers and manufacturers is surely an insult to our intelligence. As far as I can make out, nobody in England wants a 3-litre limit on Group 6 cars – neither do Ferrari or Porsche, for that matter. Surely this is another case of playing into the hands of the opposition. Instead we should have had someone expressing our views at the CSI meeting when this decision was taken.

'The drivers of works Fords, Ferraris and Chaparrals who ran at Le Mans have never been consulted as to what is dangerous about the present lack of capacity limit. The effect of limiting the capacity to 3 litres will not make the cars appreciably slower, if slower at all, and as long as the pits at Le Mans and Reims remain in their present form the danger will be there. If we had a strong enough representative putting forward the British manufacturers', owners' and drivers' points of view, they would demand in the interests of safety that something be done before there is a bloody great accident.

'If the 3-litre limit is adopted it will completely prohibit private entrants taking part in long-distance racing because of enormously increased cost. Sure, you can enter a Group 4 car up to 5 litres; you will get next to no starting money anyway, and where can you hope to finish against expensive machinery which the new formula will encourage? Motor racing has enough problems and is difficult enough without having your own representative taking the wrong decision and not consulting you before doing so.

'Why can't we have a representative body selected by the drivers and entrants and the major motor clubs to control our business effectively and intelligently?'

Not only were the regulations of motor racing about to change, but their economics were already changing dramatically. Just as Paul had begun to reap the advantages of his effort over the years, he was not a happy bunny as start money now came under threat and circuits rearranged their financial structures.

Silverstone in July was an excellent example, when with a holed piston in his GT40 he completed just four laps to earn the princely sum of £16. It didn't even cover the cost of a new piston, never mind the entrance fees, transport, fuel and wages. He needed to be looking elsewhere, and logic seemed to suggest that it would be the bigger organizations that would survive the planned changes better. Meanwhile, there was nothing for it but to bite the bullet and get on with the business that he now knew so well – driving racing cars.

Paul again in *Autosport*: 'Between these Continental races I had been racing my own Group 4 GT40 Ford in England and winning a few events, and I also took it over to Clermont-Ferrand for the Auvergne Trophy. I was trying new tyres in a wet practice session and I came downhill, turned into a corner, but the car just slid straight ahead up over a bank, and down the side of a mountain. That gave me a fright I can tell you! Fortunately it came to rest against a tree before it had skidded very far down, but we had to borrow the local tow-truck to haul it back on to the road after practice. It wasn't too badly damaged luckily and I was able to get it ready for the race.

'I wasn't able to stay with Beltoise in the 2-litre Matra, which was ideally suited to the circuit, but fortunately for me he couldn't get the car started again when he stopped for fuel, so I was able to make up a lot of ground and win the race. But I never would have done so if Beltoise hadn't had engine trouble. The GT40 is a very good motor car to race. It goes where you put it in corners, and the engine and gearbox certainly aren't as noisy as the Porsche. I've been very pleased with my car, and I would reckon that it's easily the best homologated Group 4 sports car available today.'

Having occasionally undertaken testing with Team Lotus, and with Graham Hill away for a couple of races, he was up for a drive at Silverstone, where he again bumped into his old mate Vic Elford. Vic: 'He was driving for Colin Chapman in the Lotus Cortina in the British Touring Car Championship and I was driving a Porsche 911, and we had some great races together. In fact it was the first time he had driven the 'new' version of the Lotus Cortina. It was Grand Prix weekend and I remember we were parked on the inner runways and we got back to our respective pit/garage area and were side-by-side. I got out of the car, Paul gets out of the Lotus, and Chapman came over and says: 'Well, Paul, how was the car?' And Paul started swearing...and he didn't stop for two minutes and he never repeated himself once in telling Chapman what he thought of the car.' Interestingly, he had just taken a class win, fourth overall and set a new class record, so it would seem there was limited cause for complaint, unless perhaps he still harboured a dislike of tin-tops from his days in South Africa.

Paul continues: 'The BOAC race at Brands Hatch was the last event in the prototype manufacturers' world championship, and since the Lola I had driven at Reims was being shipped to Australia for a 12-hour sports car race there, I managed to arrange a works Ferrari drive with team manager Franco Lini. It was the first time I'd driven a prototype Ferrari, and that V12 engine certainly inspires confidence. You start it up and 24 hours later it will still be sounding exactly the same. The car I was sharing with Jonathan Williams was a P4 with a 4-litre engine on fuel injection. The throttle control was beautiful. We tried all sorts of suspension settings for Brands Hatch bumps, and finally decided to set the cars up as high as they would go to avoid bottoming. It was great working with a team like Ferrari because they would try anything you suggested if it was reasonably constructive. There was never any argument and you were never told: "We've tried that before and it doesn't work". Eventually we had set the cars up to handle well. It wasn't the ideal circuit to run a P4 on – it would have been a lot happier at Silverstone or Snetterton in England, or Reims or Le Mans in France, where the car would have a chance to get into its stride.

'Surtees made off with the lead at the start and I followed him, taking over in front when he had trouble with the Lola, and I led for eight laps until the track started to get oily and the car began oversteering. I backed off then because there was 500 miles of racing to go, and there was no point in caning the car at that stage. It was very hot in the cockpit, and when I came in for the first fuel stop *Ing* Forghieri (Ferrari's team manager) smashed off the side windows. This improved the circulation, and cured our personal overheating problem.

'Denny Hulme led in his Lola until he had engine trouble, and then the Chaparral took command of the race, with the factory P4 driven by Chris Amon and Jackie Stewart in second place, which was what Ferrari wanted as the championship depended on Ferrari beating Porsche in this last race – and there was a Porsche lying third! The Porsches didn't have to stop as often as we did for fuel or tyres, but Chris and Jackie held second place, and we were fourth when I was signalled to catch the third-placed Porsche. But I must have tried too hard because I slid on the grass at Clearways, spun twice, and clipped the bank with the tail. This loosened the hinges and clips and I was doing a slow lap to come into the pits for a check over when the tail blew off. I then had to do another lap without the tail to retrieve it, fit it on again, and drive back to the pits one-handed holding the tail on with the other! This lost us quite a lot of time, and we finally finished sixth. But as Ford's ambition had been to win Le Mans, it was Ferrari's aim to beat Porsche at Brands. This they did and won the Championship.'

Yet again history was about to repeat itself and in the same way that his GT40 was currently influencing his life, the beautiful P4 Ferrari he had just driven in the BOAC 500 was about to metamorphose into a CanAm car. They would meet again.

Two weeks later at Karlskoga, his GT40 was down 1500rpm as worn lobes on the camshaft meant some rare start money and an early retirement, but just one week later at Zeltweg, with its engine hurriedly rebuilt in far from ideal conditions, he would both win the Austrian Grand Prix and set a new lap record despite losing second gear. He was not only winning, but clearly able to demonstrate he was now fully capable of driving through a car's problems, a fact that would be reinforced in the last race of the *Autosport* series at Cheshire's Oulton Park, where on lap five he broke a rocker stud, depriving the storming V8 of a cylinder, and forcing him to tactically compensate as the 250 LMs of David Piper and Richard Attwood crawled all over him in their desperate dance to overtake. The pressure showed, as the trio ducked and dived, but with Paul hanging on to a slender lead, he incredibly set yet another lap record on just seven cylinders. The three charging protagonists crossed the line within a mere 0.6 of a second of each other, enough for 'Hawkeye' to win not just the race, but the Championship. As his trophy was presented by three-times World Champion Jack Brabham, himself having just won the Gold Cup race, Paul gratefully muttered that he had 'never been so glad to see the chequered flag in my life'.

The Oulton Park race had taken place shortly after his return from Australia, where again with Jackie and the 'International' car, they had taken an improved second place in the Surfers Paradise 12-Hours. Jackie now agreed to sell the Lola to Paul, though before returning for further races 'downnunda', he had an appointment in Stockholm, where the Ford Motor Company's Advanced Vehicles (*aka* John Wyer Automotive) were looking for some experienced help to finalize their team for the forthcoming year. With Jacky Ickx away undertaking a Formula Two race, Paul took the JWA Mirage to second place, earning a drive in the forthcoming Paris 1000 Kms and thereby not only rounding off a remarkable season, but achieving a remarkable triple.

In 1967 he had driven for all three of the major contestants of the Manufacturers' Championship – Porsche, Ferrari and Ford. He had won the Targa Florio, the *Autosport* Championship, the Austrian Grand Prix, the Auvergne Trophy, and he was about to team up with Jacky Ickx to win the 1000 Kms at Montlhéry. With eight wins and five seconds to his credit so far, he had scored more Group 4/6 wins than any other driver in any other team that year, factory or otherwise, and he had driven a remarkable crop of machinery in the process.

There was his own Group 4 GT40, the 7-litre GT40 Mk 2, a 5.7-litre Mirage, Porsche 910/8 and 910/6, Ferrari P4, Lola T70 5.9-litre and Lotus Cortinas. He had raced across three continents and a host of countries including England, America, France, Italy, Germany, Sweden, Austria, and was about to pop back to Australia, where he had been engaged by Murray Wright's PR man Paul Higgins to drive an Alfa Romeo GTV in the Bathurst 500 at the Mount Panorama circuit.

If the Melbourne Cup could bring sporting Australia to a standstill, then the Bathurst race was not far behind in influence. As the Blue Riband of Australian motorsports, Aussies were increasingly aware of the battle developing between local manufacturers, and since the arrival of the race from Phillip Island in '63 the magic of the '500' had woven its web over the entire continent.

Both Ford and General Motors were now fully cognizant of its impact on the sale of their products, and over the next decade they would set out to produce vehicles that not only sold in the showrooms, but were capable of mixing the mustard along Mount Panorama's Conrod Straight. For the first time in history, home-grown machinery was seen to be truly challenging exotically priced imports, and whoever won at Bathurst could count on moving an awful lot of vehicles from their forecourts the following week. Big Aussie V8 saloons were the way to go, and importers of European sports saloons now found themselves participating in a crucible in which they were obliged to prove their worth.

It was also a time when the success of Jack Brabham had riveted the country, and with his World Championships and home-grown Repco-powered cars, he had raised motorsport's profile to new heights throughout Australia. With the Targa Florio and the *Autosport* Championship now hanging on his belt, 'Hawkeye' was beginning to be seen as a potential usurper of Brabham's crown, and great things were expected.

The 3.8-mile Mount Panorama circuit itself was, and remains, a cracker. Set on the side of a parkland hill outside the nearby town of Bathurst, competitors first pass along Pit Straight before climbing anti-clockwise up the Mountain and into the cutting. Winding up to cross the hill along Panorama Straight, it then passes across the skyline before sweeping into the accurately named Dipper and Esses, dropping downhill on to the mile-long Conrod Straight, where in the late-Sixties it enabled competitors to hit speeds never before thought possible in what were essentially showroom cars. Heavy braking to wash off the excess speed, and into a left-hander at the end of Conrod brought them back into Pit Straight, and the lap was complete. It was then, and remains today, a fabulous track for both drivers and spectators.

Teamed with Syd Fisher, the pair pushed their GTV hard in the early stages, past the gaggle of Ford Falcon GTs and into the lead, though they were obliged to watch helplessly as the other two GTVs entered by Alec Mildren slowed with problems. Their wheels were working loose as, unlike their own car, paint had not been dispersed at the nut and disc contact areas.

Regulations required driver changes, at which time they refuelled, and again they held position strongly until a stone reportedly holed their radiator and they were forced to slow. Murray Wright, however, recalls events differently, attributing their slowed progress to 'the usual heat rise Alfa problem'. Although they finished a respectable fourth in Class E, to enable an Alfa team second, the real fun had been in showing a clean set of wheels to the Fords for a time, but it was the local V8 iron, the Falcon GTs, that would take the outright victory, and a new era had dawned.

The Lola was now shipped off to South Africa, where Paul spent his time preparing it above the Johannesburg-based Williams Hunt Motors, though not without some willing assistance from the proprietor's son and his mate Howard Robinson, who recalls: 'We would go every lunch time to watch the progress. Hawkins had about three weeks to assemble this car, and my recollection is that apart from the times when the large components were put in, (*e.g.* engine, gearbox) he built the whole car himself, working on his own during long days.'

Typically, Paul reflected his own experiences in his relations with the youthful pair. 'At all times he was more than kind to us youngsters and allowed us to help with some bolts and make tea, wash pieces, measure things, etc', concludes Howard.

Meanwhile, as Paul had already made his own arrangements for the Springbok series, his new employer John Wyer was obliged to find a replacement to drive alongside Jacky Ickx in the Mirage at the opening nine-hour race at Kyalami. Brian Redman was his choice, and the pair would lead Paul and his four-times South African Champion partner John Love across the line by a margin of 13 laps as their Alan Smith engine gave unexpected problems.

Cape Town a fortnight later saw a comfortable win from David Piper's P4 Ferrari, but the Rhodesian GP meeting in early December would prove to be far from successful, generating ripples that would echo long after the event. In the Grand Prix Paul would drive John Love's Cooper T79, coming to a boiling halt after just eight laps, but it was the 20-lap sports car race that had the cat among the pigeons, creating mayhem.

The Lola, having been repaired since its outing at the Kyalami Nine-Hours, was leading the 20-lap race and looking every inch a winner until it stopped on lap 10 with zero oil pressure. An inspection found cotton wool in the oil tank, and Paul could be heard yelling 'sabotage' very loudly indeed amongst his usual oaths and blasphemies. Acrimony flew up, down and sideways, and by the end of the year the secretary of the Bulawayo Motor Sport Association was calling Paul's claim 'a blatant lie', by which time Paul's Lola had scored another win in the Laurenco Marques three-hour race, and was now sharing the Championship lead with Group 4 GT40 pilot Ed Nelson.

The importance of that lost place at Bulawayo could now be clearly evaluated, as they equally held two wins and a second place in their respective classes. However, as Ed had taken a class first in the longer Kyalami race against Paul's second in that event, it counted for more, and Paul not only needed to win the final race, but also hope that Ed's GT40 would fall off the island. The Championship would go down to the wire at the Dickie Dale three-hours race at Pietmaritzburg's Roy Hesketh circuit.

The race was brilliant as Paul, yet again driving the demanding three hours unassisted, diced dramatically with the Lola of Serrurier and Pretorius until just 10 minutes from the end of the race, when his Chevvy engine spat the dummy, throwing a pair of conrods through the block and blowing up in the most convincing way possible. This let the GT40 of Mike Hailwood and Ed Nelson into second place on the road, though as they already led their class, any hopes Paul had of the Championship had evaporated with the oil of his engine.

According to the regulations, the fact that Paul had not crossed the finish line meant he was unclassified, but he created a stink, protesting to the organizers, who asked Nelson and Hailwood to allow him second place in the Championship as it made no difference to anyone except Paul.

As with Bathurst, he would return, but not before he had bumped into a young South African called Richie Bray. Richie fancied becoming a motorsport mechanic, to which Paul in his usual blunt manner said: 'You get a work permit, and I'll give you a job'. It was as simple as that, and all settled. Both were men of their word. His final *Autosport* quip sums up this most extraordinary of years. 'All in all I've had quite a busy old time.'

Chapter Nine

I've got to get out of this place

Lynton Garage, Fortis Green, London N2 was, at least from the front, a perfectly normal garage apart from the passageway down the middle with its row of lockups and overhead bridge. Paul Hawkins Racing had been based here for some time now, and at the beginning of 1968 there were a number of folk using these garages, the last six of which had originally been Ian Walker's and were now occupied by Roger Nathan and his partner Cedric Selzer. Others were used by David Piper, whose Ferraris had been frequent winners in South Africa, whilst GP Metalcraft continued its lucrative, if noisy business shaping and developing bodywork for its market namesake, and John Etheridge sublet from Paul, making space for his Aston Martin.

Paul's team was now composed of people whom he both knew and trusted. Richie Bray had by now joined him from South Africa, whilst Betty Biles fulfilled everything from her official role of administrator/secretary to general gofer and occasional landlady. Her phone engineer boyfriend Martin might just as well have been part of the team, for he was frequently helping out around the garage, and on the whole the team gelled brilliantly, led by Paul's exuberant style.

'He was loud', recalls John Etheridge. 'He always had a grin and a laugh, and he liked a joke and a good time. Before you actually saw Paul come through, you would hear him.' And by now he was well-known not only in motor racing circles, but increasingly publicly also, for he had achieved the pinnacle of so many racers in that era – a factory drive with a major international team. Journalists jostled for interviews, and his fame was spreading fast. He wasn't, however, one to let it go to his head, and he would always be there for a mate. Straight down the line.

His GT40, however – a design that was several years old – was now beginning to struggle against more modern machinery, and after fitting 14-inch wheels, wider arches and a few other modifications he again set his sights at the *Autosport* Championship, while keeping his eye as usual on the occasional sideline profit. In this last matter, he concluded that there was money to be had in dealing in GT40s (even advising others to get in on the act), and he set about acquiring the means to turn metal into money, whilst happily and coincidentally expanding his team to two cars.

Jackie Epstein advised caution in his venture because of his existing sponsorship deals with Castrol and Firestone, but Paul wouldn't hear of it and promptly set about purchasing a second GT40 in chassis 1019. But there remained more yet. Having sold his Lola to Mike de Udy, Paul then sat down for a beer and a chat with his mate Stan, who just happened to be looking after a bunch of Ford bits and pieces at their Yeovil Road yard – bits which happened to include an early experimental GT40.

John Etheridge recalls: 'It was a car I believe Stan was not supposed to sell. He (Paul) didn't want John Wyer or John Horsman, or any people to know he was buying it, otherwise he would never have got the car, but Paul used to love this guy, saying: 'Stan, is there anything you need to tell me?'. The bean counters at JWA were soon wondering just who it was that had managed to whisk the car out from under their noses, for no-one in motor racing had ever heard of the name on the cheque. Whether it was Betty or Martin's name that appeared, it would take them quite a while to establish that GT105 was now parked up, safe and sound, as a spares supply at Fortis Green, and Paul Hawkins Racing Ltd was now a two-car team in the peripheral business of renting out GT40s to those who could afford the going rate.

While the Daytona 24-Hours would be his third drive for JWA, the March event would be the opener of the 1968 Championship of Makes, and with Paul teamed with David Hobbs in chassis 1074, Brian Redman and Jacky Ickx would drive in sister car 1075. If anything, Jacky at 23 was the youngster of the team and he recalls of Paul: 'He was a funny person with a lot of character and a big sense of humour, and an Australian accent as good as mine in French-speaking English. Very attractive...a big sense of humour. At the time he was reckoned as a talented person. Someone with a lot of experience, as David was. I was the youngest one. I was the kid in the team, because I was very young really...and they were already famous people.' Certainly there was a considerable age difference, for by now Paul was knocking on the door of 31, while David was just a couple of years younger – though age was never an issue when it came to Paul's enjoyment.

'It must have been the night before the race,' recalls David Hobbs. 'Anyway, we were driving the GT40. We went to this reception, and Paul let off one of his favourite fireworks, so that got us thrown out of there. Then somebody thought it was me, so I got it in the neck (sounds a familiar story!). Anyway, we sort of left there and went down the beach, which is now totally built-up, and we went to some restaurant down there – a divey sort of a place. Well, of course, he lets off another one of these M80s under the waitress' legs, so she screamed blue murder and says she's been burned and attacked and the next thing we're running across the road and getting in our car and driving off from there as well. I think we must have gone on somewhere else because on the morning of the race old Paul comes out of his room and he says: "Jeezes Christ, my f***ing head, it's killing me".'

Needless to say, it wasn't the most auspicious start to a 24-hour race, but by now Paul had more than enough practice to be able to face a drive with a hangover. David: 'In the race we ended up leading quite handily, because Brian had spun the other car. While it was still going backwards he let the clutch out – it absolutely fried the clutch in a heartbeat. So Paul and I and the Porsches were strong. Vic Elford was in a Porsche with Jochen Neerpasch and a bunch of guys (including Paul's other 'oppo' Stommelen). They were all humming along, but they started to have troubles with the 908s, and the next thing is we're leading. We led for a long time, and then I came in for a pit stop at about seven o'clock in the morning and it wasn't a scheduled driver change.

'I'm sitting in the car, and they're putting the fuel in and team manager David Yorke signals me out. So I get out and I'm wondering what the hell's going on, and bloody fuel was pouring out underneath the car as quick as it was going in. They'd failed to line the inside of the monocoque where the rivets were so it didn't rub on the bag tank. Somebody had failed to do that! It just leaked fuel out of the bag tank.'

There was one small crumb to be saved from the event, though, for in practice JWA had begun a process of technical recording that represented the dawning of today's high-tech monitoring systems, and had fitted a Taplin meter to the cars to record the driver's pedal action. Paul would later proudly recount that he was the only driver not to lift off on the high-speed banking. It might not have been the most successful event from the team's viewpoint, but it had certainly provided an opportunity for Paul to demonstrate his spherical attributes to best effect.

A month later, Sebring would explode Paul's name around the world. Needless to say, it would be his mouth that would firmly put his foot into the squishy stuff, but he never cared much about that anyway as he was always one for saying what he thought; fair and square. Teamed still with David, they had steadily moved from seventh on the grid, working their way up to race-leading position when, after eight hours of solid racing, 'Hawkeye' clipped a 911.

The Porsche he smacked had swerved into his path avoiding

a Rambler driven by Liane Engerman and Janet Guthrie, and Paul as ever said it as he saw it: 'It was not the Porsche's fault. It was those bloody girls in a Javelin. They drove like they were going to a funeral!' He certainly used some other 'Hawkeye Specials', and David recalls that he was very complimentary about 'bloody women on the bloody f***ing race track...should be in the kitchen', and all that sort of stuff.' He wasn't happy, and really let rip. As the Javelin had been second slowest in practice (to a Spitfire) he may have had a point, but the press pack seized their opportunity and as next morning's tabloid headlines blared 'Bloody Women Drivers' across the UK, Paul immediately became the ostracized target of half the world's driving population.

April 7th would see the first outing of Paul's second team car (GT40 1019), which won the Barcelona Six-Hours with Muir and Godia, while Paul would take a fourth with David in his own car at Brands on the same day that a shocked racing world would stand, stunned, by the news of Jimmy Clark's death at Hockenheim.

Motor racing was still highly dangerous, and the changes that would engender a much safer environment were only just beginning to influence the sport. Today, decades later, it is perhaps difficult to appreciate the realities of that risk, for though at that time seat belts were in use, Paul and his compatriots were still unaware that crutch belts prevented the submarine effect in an accident; never mind the fact that when compared to the chassis of today, cars of the era were far more prone to breakage and fire.

At Monza, on April 25th, the circuit organizers were at least trying to minimize the potential dangers of their famous banking. David Hobbs recalls that it was probably the very last time that the combined road and banked circuits were used, and measures had been taken to slow the cars. 'The track was so wide from the pits that you went down the inside by the pit lane and down to a chicane, went up on to the banking, round it, and off the banking on to another chicane. They didn't want us going round the banking flat-out 'cos it was pretty dodgy even then,' he says, and for cars capable of 200 miles an hour, the inclusion of the chicanes was a wise precaution.

The Wyer team as usual were fielding their two 4.7-litre Group 4 GT40s, on this occasion in identical race trim, and whilst it was the first time that Paul and David had driven this version of the circuit, they were soon placed second behind flying team-mates Ickx and Redman, closely followed by the rest of the 35-car grid, including a pair of 3-litre prototype Porsches and a mixed bag of privateer GT40s, Porsches and Alfa Tipo 33s. In fact, Paul's Targa-winning Porsche 910 from the previous year was also there, on this occasion being driven by his old mate Vic Elford, while his Targa 'oppo' Stommelen would drive a 907.

The start immediately set the scene for a Porsche/Ford punch-up as Siffert and Scarfiotti's prototype 908s were closely hounded by Jacky, with Paul in fourth. By lap four Jacky had thrown down the gauntlet and taken the lead, only to have Paul slipstream past all three of them on the straight. The four leaders steadily pulled out a lead, and the race developed into a series of slipstreaming manoeuvres on the fast circuit, as first Porsche, then Ford took the lead, and by lap 10 there were a mere seven seconds between the four leading cars as they pulled yet further from the pack. On lap 15, oil became a problem and Paul slowed as it covered both the track and his screen, as shortly after Siffert's Porsche pitted, trailing its own personal smokescreen. With Jacky well out in front, the race order suddenly changed, as first Scarfiotti fell out with ignition difficulties, followed by leader Ickx with a split exhaust. Paul rushed into the lead, with Stommelen's 907 in hot pursuit, and by lap 30 the pair were the best part of two minutes ahead of David Piper, leading the remaining chase. Brian Redman now brought the other JWA car back into the fray on lap 34, but had by now lost seven laps on his Hawkins/Hobbs team-mates.

On lap 40, with David having taken over from Paul, their GT40 was leading the Stommelen 907 by an increased margin of more than four minutes, while Brian Redman desperately sought to make up time. However, just past the halfway mark, Brian spun his car, pitting again with a split exhaust that signalled the end of his race. Shortly after this David also pitted, his engine having unexpectedly cut out, and a leaking fuel tank was the prime suspect. Refuelled, Paul took the car back into the lead, eventually taking the chequered flag from the Stommelen/Neerpasch 907, though not before some last-minute high drama as once again the big Ford's engine spluttered for want of fuel, and only the lightning work of the pit crew got them back in front. Needless to say, following DNFs at Daytona and Sebring, John Wyer was much happier. With Monza in the bag alongside the win Jacky and Brian had given them at Brands, Ford were beginning to close the gap in the Championship.

In the background, Paul had been quietly beavering away within his team for the support necessary for a solitary Targa entry, but the issue of start money would foil the attempt to repeat his previous year's win; though in truth the big Ford was probably not the most appropriate of entries for the winding, mountainous course. Meanwhile, back in the UK with his own car, he was managing to keep up the pressure within the *Autosport* Championship, and the fourth at Brands was soon followed with a second at Oulton and a third at Silverstone, while his new driving partner Eric Liddell took the now dark blue 1019 car to third behind Paul's first at Zandvoort.

Business at the Lynton Rd garage was brisk, not that Paul was into over-working himself if he didn't need to. More often than not he would turn up at six in the evening ready for a trip down to the Isle of Dogs, where after a sing-song and a few pints of his favourite nectar he would stir up customers in the *Waterman's Arms*. Paddy Driver recalls: 'Pub crawling with Hawkins was an exciting escapade. His penchant was to get an argument going in a pub in which two opposing parties would become very vehement with each other, losing sight of the fact that he was the instigator of what usually became a fracas. At this point he would give me the wink and say "time to leave", and we used to sneak out, leaving a heaving, arguing mass of people behind. And, of course, off to another pub we would go and start the whole business again.'

For all his larrikin escapades, though, he was really well liked, as his enthusiasm and huge friendliness melted all before him. Off the track he really was one of the boys – gregarious, outgoing, and a bloody good mate to have around; though with his rugby player build and sheer physical strength, you wouldn't want to be the one to cross him.

The Nürburgring in May was a well-known quantity to Paul, the race this time taking place just a matter of days after his old Walker team-mate Mike Spence had been killed in practice at Indianapolis. As usual, the show would go on.

Paul had driven the 'Ring on numerous occasions, and prior to his win in the Targa he had rated it as his favourite circuit. John Wyer was well aware of the fact, and as it was Brian Redman's first visit, he elected to pair the experienced 'Hawkeye' with Jacky in 1074 on this occasion. For whatever reason it was an unwise choice, and Paul would be unable to match Jacky's pace, while Brian Redman would excel on the classic circuit. Porsche would take the first two places, leaving Jacky and Paul with third while David, paired with Brian, came in eighth.

May also meant Spa, and with their usual chassis away for refit, Paul and David, back together as usual, were given 1084 to drive with its new 4.9-litre engine. Paul, however, was as much interested in finding a certain cartoonist, who had (as far as Paul was concerned) produced a most unflattering caricature of his rough-hewn face following the Sebring incident, and he stomped around the paddock in poor humour.

The esteemed motor racing journalist and author Doug Nye was over there to cover the 1000 Kms race and recalls his encounter with 'Hawkeye': 'The offending cartoon, by Don Grant, whose style was somewhat reminiscent of Gerald Scarfe's, had been used to illustrate an article on Paul being run in *Speedworld International*, a new magazine which had just been launched by Don's father, Gregor Grant, who in 1950 had been the founder of *Autosport*.

'Hawkeye' was really steaming and in full flow. He button-holed me and said: "D'you know this f***ing Grant? If I get hold o' the bastard I'll stick his f***ing pencils up his f***ing arse and shove his sharpener up there too…and his f***ing magazine, and his f***ing drawing board if it'll f***ing fit! I know I'm no f***ing oil painting, but that's not the f***ing problem. It's one thing to have a 'f***ing laugh at someone else's expense, but this is just f***ing takin' the f***ing piss, and I don't f***ing see why I should be f***ing expected to put the f*** up with it."

'He finished up with a very rude word which pretty much rounded-out his opinion at the time of the perfectly nice Mr Grant and his talented artistry; I came to the conclusion that he had just awarded him a decisive 'No' vote.'

Returning to the matter in hand at Spa, and deciding that the new engine was down on power, the pair chose to stay with the tried and tested 4.7-litre unit, which in the race suffered from failing oil pressure to leave them in fourth place on the rain-drenched and steaming circuit. Behind them at the end of the race was the Ferrari P4 of Scarfiotti/Parkes, but Ludovico Scarfiotti, one of sports car racing's greatest, would not be returning to Spa. Just a few days later he died while competing at the Rossfeld hill-climb.

Back again to Lynton Rd garage, it was time to pick up the red car for a disappointing double-header race at the Norisring, where in front of a crowd of 60,000 people, and lying in fourth place, the car broke a bypass hose, leaving Paul officially finishing in 15th place. Repaired, he and his crew then began the week-long journey across a Europe of few motorways to Vila Real, in Portugal, where one of the last road races of the traditional kind was about to be run. The track itself wound through local townships and along mountainous public roads round the Mateus vineyards, and strong competition was guaranteed. Peter Jackson, remembered from his days with Sprinzel, was now campaigning a Lotus 47 in long-distance races.

'In some ways this period was a golden age of motorsport,' he says. 'Those of us who were privileged to take part were a close-knit crowd who travelled around the continent with a very assorted collection of support vehicles, collecting our starting money and moving from meeting to meeting like a band of nomads. At the minor end of the field we could just about make ends meet. Those like Paul, at the front of the grid with the heavy metal, were probably making quite a good living out of it, but we all had a lot of fun.

'I remember very vividly the six-hour race at Vila Real in Portugal, where we were sharing the same garage as Paul. On the way down we had a very scary moment with our trailer, which was pretty old and basic and not too stable. We had got into a very violent snaking situation whilst trying to overtake another outfit on a narrow tree-lined road. I mentioned this to Paul. "No problem, mate, I'll soon fix that. What you need is a bit more toe-in." Whereupon he gets out the welding gear and jack, heats the solid axle on the trailer to a glowing red, and duly gives it a bit of toe-in. Problem solved! Good old Paul, one of the stars of the meeting, but not too busy to give a helping hand to an old friend.'

In practice, Paul's engine would expire in a rather dramatic fashion, leaving him to fit a spare that did not benefit from the usual Weslake tweeks, and in the race he had to settle for third, while Eric in the blue car managed seventh. That same day, Jo Schlesser would crash in the French Grand Prix at Rouen, and motor racing would claim yet another young life.

Back in Portugal, still blissfully unaware of the sad news, Paul had already taken advantage of the rather good local wine just waiting for his entrepreneurial talents. Peter Jackson continues: 'The Mateus Palace was in the centre of the circuit, and in those days the local Mateus Rose was very fashionable. Somewhere along the line, Paul had managed to do a deal to acquire a considerable quantity of this wine, and being a good wheeler-dealer he was busy off-loading some of this to all the other competitors. I remember that he offered us some, but being short of funds and also space, as the old Austin 110 tow car was already bursting at the seams, we declined. However, a number of people did take up the offer, and on the return trip to England the first transporter arrived at customs.

"Anything to declare, Sir?"

"No."

So customs start to search and find 50 bottles of Mateus Rose. A certain amount of difficulty ensues.

Next transporter arrives. "Anything to declare, Sir?"

"No."

Customs search and find 100 bottles of Mateus Rose, leading to considerably more difficulty.

Paul arrives with his battered old coach. "Anything to declare, Sir?"

"Yes, mate, five bottles of wine and a bottle of port".

Customs: "You're the first honest man through here today."

Paul: "Cheers, mate", and drives off with 300 bottles of Mateus under the floorboards.

That was Paul's great charm. He was so outrageous at times that he could get away with murder.'

In the post-race party, however, his charm didn't quite have the intended result. Peter: 'We had a very good party, during which Paul produced some shark scarers (M80s, as usual) which livened up the night quite a bit, and resulted in him and David Piper relinquishing their passports.'

This was just a bit worrying, as the six-hour race at Watkins Glen was just one week away, and he'd not only to get the cars back to Fortis Green, but catch a plane to the USA *and* practice the car. The Portuguese police eventually relented and their charge of 'conspiring to cause explosions', outside the local police station of all places, was eventually dropped.

However, relationships within the Wyer team would begin to change for Paul at Watkins Glen. It wasn't as if there was open enmity between the two cars and their drivers, in fact they generally saw very little of each other apart from turning up for testing and racing, and they all related well to each other, even if they didn't live in each other's pockets. However, it seemed to David in particular that Jacky Ickx benefited from a bit of John Wyer favouritism, with which Jacky agrees in at least part, saying: 'Let's say I was at least as fast as the others.' As Jacky in the number-one car had in fact set fastest time for the team on all four occasions to date, it seems the most likely reason for his being high on John Wyer's Christmas list.

Certainly the individualistic attitude expected of racers in any competitive sport showed through, and from Jacky's point of view, he, like everyone else in the team, was out to win. In the same way that 'Hawkeye' and Frank Gardner had been friendly rivals in their time together with Willment, Jacky also found his thoughts focused on the issue, later confirming his favoured position within the team, saying that what really mattered was down simply to who was fastest. In achieving that ultimate goal it would, of course, be his co-driver who mattered more than any other team-mates. 'You can only make a relationship with someone who uses the same car as you,' he would suggest. 'As I was leading Brian, he was leading David, in his car anyhow. Obviously the boss of his car from my point of view.' At international level, that competitiveness so often apparent between team-mates would also be influenced by team perception, and team orders that were difficult to ignore.

Yet again Jacky would set the faster time in practice at the Glen, on this occasion teamed with Lucien Bianchi, and on race day, after just three-quarters of an hour, the blue and orange Gulf-sponsored cars had already begun to show a clean pair of heels to the chasing Porsches. Sixty laps in, and David in the number-two car was lying in second place, a lap behind Jacky, and at the two-hour mark, in unchanged position, they pitted for driver changes.

Porsche meanwhile suffered catastrophe on top of calamity as one by one their challenges evaporated, whilst out in front Lucien Bianchi in Jacky's car was experiencing oil pressure problems and was obliged to slow. Paul in the number-two car was now breathing down his neck and going like a train, but he was given the 'hold' sign and ordered to stay in position. Four and a half hours into the six-hour race, Paul finally got past as Bianchi's tyre burst, and he soon developed a two-lap lead. The next driver change saw David relieve Paul, where he picks up the story.

'We were leading by miles, and then the team wanted Ickx to win. Not that it made any difference to the World Championship or anything. There were no drivers' points as such, but they just wanted Ickx to win, and we had a lap lead. I mean, this was about my first really good major drive for a major team. And Wyer and David Yorke were putting out signs – 'Go slow...Go slow...Easy...Easy'.

Round the first corner and out of sight of their pit, Paul and Richard Attwood were hanging over the fence at the edge of the track, egging David on and screaming their lungs out for him to ignore the team order. David: 'I kept trying to go reasonably fast without absolutely spitting in the face of the team, but at the same time...' In the end, of course, Jacky caught him up and passed to take the win.

'It was a bitter pill to swallow,' says David. 'The even worse thing was that he'd had low oil pressure for practically the whole race and he just drove like an absolute man possessed. Anybody else and the bloody engine would have just blown up. The night after the race, we stayed at the *Glen Motor Court*. David Yorke had a hell of a row with me, ripping into me. He got very cross because I had dared to not slow down when he told me to.

'The day after, we were at the airport down at Elmira, which is the little airport we flew into, and the Gulf people were there. Grady Davis was the big boss, and they had their own jet there – a Lear, or a Gulfstream or something – and we were about to catch a regular plane back to New York to come back to England. And these guys met us in the lobby. They gave us a thousand dollars each. They said: 'Y'know, it should never have happened. You guys got screwed by the team.'

The result at Watkins Glen was disappointing, and Paul had

driven with Jacky as a team-mate for the last time. Now he was looking in other directions, as David Hobbs continues: 'It was a fairly hierarchical team. Wyer wasn't the sort of guy who was going to take lip from anybody...and nor was Paul. He was a very spirited type of guy, and he was a pretty cool operator. He was much more of a wheeler-dealer than I ever was...and I don't think he liked driving for other people unless he had some control. With Wyer, you had no control. John Wyer, John Horsman and David Yorke were all very team-orientated, and I don't think Paul looked at it very favourably at all.'

The World Sportscar Championship would go down to the wire at Le Mans later in September, where JWA would field three cars. Meanwhile, the *Autosport* Championship continued, and at Oulton Park in August Paul would take third place in Ulf Norinder's borrowed Lola, though the real issue on this occasion was a chance conversation with Kiwi Chris Amon, who mentioned a Ferrari for sale back in Australia.

Paul promptly phoned team principal David McKay, of *Scuderia Veloce*, in Sydney, just beating David Piper to the deal, and from this time onwards his busy lifestyle would go into overdrive. The spares mule GT40 he had acquired from Ford was now put up for sale, and Paul could be heard repeatedly banging on about the poor income to be had from racing in the UK.

Certainly the *Autosport* final at Brands Hatch didn't help much, for Bill Bradley in his 2-litre Porsche was ahead on points in his class and Paul was the only other driver with the mathematical potential to beat him. While he had substantially modified AMGT2, updating the suspension and bodywork in his efforts to remain competitive, there was little doubt that the four-year-old car was nearing the end of its life as a front runner. Other than the factory cars, it was often Eric Broadley's Lolas that were taking the laurels in UK races, and to have the best chance of winning the series Paul turned to John Woolfe for help. His T70 Mk 3 GT was fitted with a Bartz 485bhp engine and a deal was done for its use in the forthcoming final. Then it all went pear-shaped.

For some inexplicable reason the engine was sent to Paris by mistake, and it is easy to imagine a few 'Hawkeye Specials' being flung around once he heard the news. There was nothing left for it but to use his ageing but faithful 'red rocket' one more time. But a puncture would seal the outcome and the now famous car slipped steadily down the field to 10th place, leaving 'Hawkeye' with 52 points to Bradley's 58.

He might have missed the Championship second time around, but he was by now the most successful GT40 privateer that had ever driven the tarmac, and it was time for Le Mans and one final fling in Ford's flying GT40.

'Le Mans was very late that year', says David Hobbs. 'It was in September because of an election or something (actually a referendum), and in practice we thought the car was vibrating a bit so we drove back to La Châtre, which is where we were garaged, to change the engine. While they were about to change it they found that the exhaust pipe, or some part of the engine, was touching the chassis, so they said: "Do you think that's what the vibration is?" Could be, you know, so we went for a drive down the road. And Paul drove. And of course there are these little country lanes round La Châtre – still are! We didn't have a speedo, obviously, but we must have been doing 150mph down these little roads and I'm sat in the passenger seat. We're both saying to each other: "Well, I don't know...maybe it does seem a bit better. Maybe that's what it was all along,".'

Choosing to leave well-enough alone, the following day was the 36th running of the *Vingt-quatre Heures du Mans*. It would be the greatest opportunity Paul would ever have to achieve a win in the classic race. He was partnered with David, on whom he knew he could depend, with a crew he knew, a car he knew, and he was fully aware of the possibility that JWA stood at least a 50/50 chance against the Porsches. It would be a three-car entry, though on this occasion without Jacky Ickx or Brian Redman as both had recently suffered injury. They would be replaced by Pedro Rodriguez and Lucien Bianchi, while a third car for the event would be piloted by fellow Aussie Brian Muir, parked alongside Brit Jackie Oliver. Paul would also have his own mechanic with him in the form of Richie Bray, on loan to the Gulf team to help bolster the additional load created by the third car.

Paul and David put their car sixth on the grid, and David recalls: 'For those Le Mans starts we used to do all sorts of silly things like hanging the seatbelts up on the ceiling so you could get in and put your arm through the belt. Of course, you did all that struggling, putting the belt on going down the road at 160mph! You needed a bit of finesse in sports cars as well, because in those days they weren't anything like as bullet-proof as they are today. In 1968, for instance, when we went, we had done something like 4 minutes, or 4 minutes 10 seconds in practice qualifying. And John Wyer said: "In the race we're going to run at (like) 4.20". Way off the pace. I mean, you didn't just go down to the hairpin and lamp on the brakes, yank it down to first and scream out of the hairpin; which is what they do now. So you did actually need a lot of finesse and at the same time you needed to be relatively aggressive with traffic, because obviously there's us doing 200 down the straight, and there's a Fiat Abarth doing 110. Of course, if you get mixed up at the hairpin or the Esses it can really bugger your lap time horribly. You had to be very judicious about the way you picked your way through the traffic. You wanted to maintain a certain pace, obviously, so you couldn't wait forever, but on the other hand you couldn't just go barging by.

'One of the problems with today's long-distance racing is there's still a pretty good speed differential between the front and the back and these days you *do* go barging by, and they're always running into these guys. We didn't used to run into those slow guys at all. It was not a huge problem. It *was* frustrating, but it was different then to what it is now.'

The grid was away at three o'clock, and on the 12th lap 'Yogi' Muir parked his car on top of a sandbank at Mulsanne, where it would stay despite his best efforts for nearly three hours. He and Jackie Oliver were clearly out of contention and would later retire, by which time the two remaining JWA cars were running together at the front, their strategy being closely adhered to.

Earlier in the race Willy Mairesse had suffered a monumental accident when his car crashed heavily on the Mulsanne in full view of Paul, who later described the remains of his car as 'seven feet long, three feet wide and eighteen inches high'. Willy would suffer a fractured skull, and the 1966 Targa Florio winner's career was virtually over.

Four hours into the race and Paul and David's number 10 car had been leading the field for some time when the clutch began to give problems, necessitating an 80-minute stop for repairs before they again flew out to resume the chase. It wasn't to last, and around midnight they would regret their previous day's decision to leave well enough alone. David: 'The bloody thing blew up, and obviously we should have changed the bloody thing. We probably could have won that one. We were going well enough to. I think Paul and I could handle Bianchi alright.'

History now records that the Rodriguez/Bianchi car would go on to win, clinching the Championship of Makes for Ford, and while it had been a team effort that had made the difference, Paul was simply too renegade to be a good team player. Unbeknown to JWA, he had been playing his own games, and against all the rules (they only existed to be broken) he had managed to smuggle a couple of girlfriends into the pits; making sure they didn't meet each other, of course. It seems that he at least enjoyed his last Le Mans.

Back at Fortis Green, inevitably, he was still up to his larrikin behaviour as Jackie Epstein recalls: 'Now, we also had another car. And when the season was over Paul said: "Matey, we're going to paint this car like the first one." And I said: "Paul, you can't do that," but he said: "Oh yes I can, matey," so he did. He painted it, and it had a pukka engine in it. It was a full race car, and he sold both cars, and to this very day the two owners argue as to which is which.'

Now, having sold AMGT2 to Spaniard Jose-Maria Juncadella, he was off to Australia to have a chat with David McKay, and another crack at Bathurst.

Chapter Ten

Everyone's gone to the moon

In Australia, David McKay's *Scuderia Veloce* had been operating successfully for some years, and the arrival of CanAm Ferrari P4 spider chassis 0858 in early '68 had given him a modern and competitive machine. This was the same P4 which Scarfiotti had taken to second place at Le Mans in '66 and which 'Hawkeye' and Jonathan Williams had driven in the BOAC 500 in '67. Since then it had been redesigned as a spider, fitted with a 4.2-litre engine and was one of a pair of Ferraris that had competed in the '67 CanAm series.

It had cost David a whopping A$30,000, and regardless of its success or otherwise in Australia, Customs would require a very heavy import tax to be paid within one year of its arrival that would very nearly double the price. The simplest way of avoiding this onerous and expensive detail was to get it out of the country within that period, which is exactly where one Robert Paul Hawkins entered the scene with his plan to ship it to South Africa for the 1968/69 Springbok series.

At the time, David was also heavily into the developing challenges of the London-to-Sydney Marathon and the Bathurst 500 on behalf of General Motors Holden, who had not only risen to the previous year's Ford bait, but had a new car in the Monaro and a fully organized dealer team to support it.

He had already planned a three-car entry for Bathurst, and it seems that with Paul on the doorstep he could not resist the opportunity of offering the experienced expat a drive. He recalls: 'I teamed Paul with Bill Brown, who was at the time driving either my LM or the P4, with mixed results, but who I thought would pair well with Paul. Paul was the easiest of drivers to manage – no *prima donna*, despite his rapid rise in sports car racing, only too willing to do whatever was asked of him, and I was sure he had a good chance of winning the race.'

Whilst GM's 327ci Monaro would indeed win the race, commencing an era of manufacturer competition that would last a decade, Paul and Bill were not so fortunate. From third on the grid they worked themselves into second position on lap 12, dropping back to fourth for much of the race, then sitting back within striking distance as the Falcon GTs slugged it out with the gaggle of Monaros. But towards race end, on lap 108, a wheel broke. Officially their 327 GTS would be disqualified for the tow back to the pits before restarting, and that was the end of their race.

Paul now handed over his money, and though he and David hadn't met before, he left a solid impression. 'I remember Paul as a typical Australian who one would have been happy to have alongside you in the trenches,' says David. 'Brave, resolute, practical; or in my case as a member of my tank crew would have suited him to a T. He was pleasant and straight-forward, and his word was his bond. In a way, Paul was like an Australian Denny Hulme, whom I also liked greatly. Decent, no-nonsense types.'

His view of Paul might have been slightly modified, however, had he been aware that he had popped down to Melbourne to see a few old mates. Here he renewed his acquaintance with George Makin, remembered from his first job at the Simca dealership. They had gone one evening to a local car club event, where Paul again resorted to his childhood prank of pinching the lighting fuse to leave them fumbling in the dark, while his smoking doughnuts in the courtesy car provided by Ford were not something the global giant really wished to know about. Some things would never change!

Now, with the Ferrari in his pocket he managed to talk mechanic Roy Pounder into accompanying him to South Africa, where Richie Bray would join them from the UK. The first race of the season would be the Kyalami Nine-Hours on November 9th, where John Love would partner him, but there was trouble ahead. The car had been freighted across from Australia, only to be landed at the wrong port, and finding all the necessary bits and pieces was proving difficult. Paul was shattered, leaving John Love to shake out the car and sort their Gunston sponsorship prior to the event, while Roy Pounder and Richie Bray got on with the job in hand.

'He had a very good way with people,' says Roy. 'He had this terrific personality where he could always get people to do work on the spur of the moment for us; particularly in South Africa. Working with him, he never got flustered when things went wrong with the car. He always managed to keep very calm. John Love was the same. They were very, very easy people to work with.'

Both Roy and Richie, of course, were up to their eyeballs preparing the car, but they all managed to find some space to relax, where Paul was once again in high spirits. Richie: 'One particular night, about a week before the race, Paul, myself, Mike Hailwood, Paddy Driver and a few of the mechanics went to a restaurant in Johannesburg. It was a fairly expensive place and we had a tie and jacket on and all the rest of it. The food was very slow coming, and we all decided to take our jackets off because it was getting very hot. So we took them off, and the food stopped. Of course, Paul called the waiter over and said: 'What's the problem?' And the waiter said: 'You've taken your jackets off, we're not going to serve you.' So Paul said (in his best English, of course) that we were going to *keep* our jackets off.

'There was a stand off as such, and Paul said that he wasn't going to eat even if he did put his jacket on. In the end they wouldn't serve us, so Paul and Mike said: "Bugger this, we're going to leave," and everybody promptly got up and walked out. But like most restaurants, you have all the *hors d'ouvres* on the table as you walk in the front door. There's always the smoked salmon and that sort of thing there, and Paul was the last one to walk out. And Paul and Mike rolled up these great big smoked salmon; they must have been 800mm long. They just rolled them up, stuffed them in their pockets, and walked out!

'Now in South Africa, even in those days, everyone was very, very security-conscious, and everywhere had steel external doors. As Paul walked out he closed the door and locked it from the outside, so as all the staff were coming round with the bill, screaming and shouting at us, Paul locked them all in.

'Paul had got a Galaxie 500, and I distinctly remember that Mike Hailwood had a yellow Iso Grifo. Mike went screaming off, and Paddy went screaming off in something or other, and of course Paul followed them, racing to the other side of Johannesburg. We came to a T-junction and Mike and Paddy had slowed up, because obviously we could only turn left, but Paul didn't realize what was happening and thought it was a straight-forward crossroads.

'Of course, he comes flying down the hill, realizes that it's a T-junction on to a motorway, locks all the wheels up, pulls out and passes the other two. We went straight across this motorway, took the Armco barrier in the middle with us, across the other side and down this big embankment. And this is not his car – this belongs to Ford in South Africa. It was absolutely rooted. We were OK, but the next thing, he's trying to get it into reverse gear and the thing is *absolutely knackered*. He turned up at Ford South Africa the following day and said: "I'm sorry, your car was pinched last night."

The *Rand Daily Mail* Nine-Hours at Kyalami was wet. It was very wet. The heavens opened, and while they were leading, the first outing of Paul Hawkins' Team Gunston expensive import was flustered by two of those bits that had previously gone walkabout. The job of the errant cover plates was to prevent water access to sensitive electrics; and they were *sodden*. The subsequent delay trying to dry everything out cost them dear, and their inability to capitalize on the Ferrari's power in the drenching torrent saw them eventually take third behind Paul's old team-mates Jacky Ickx and David Hobbs in John Wyer's Mirage, and the second-placed Dino Ferrari of Dean and van Rooyen.

Next up was the Cape Town Three-Hours, and playing the hard man as usual, he would drive it single-handed, winning in fine style from the ex-Wyer Mirage, now punted by Mike Hailwood and David Hobbs, although the real threat on this occasion was David Piper and Dickie Attwood in the former's Ferrari P4. Bulawayo was next, where he took a first and a second, though as neither race was of any great duration, they didn't count toward the series.

Mozambique, however, did, and if rain had influenced the Kyalami race, it would be sand on this occasion. With the wind whipping it across the track, it got absolutely everywhere, causing the Ferrari's throttle to stick repeatedly and forcing several stops in the three-hour race. Once again the Hailwood Mirage came through to take the win, but as always it was then party time, and Richie Bray, following his earlier escapade, was surprisingly still trusting enough to join his fun-seeking boss once more.

Richie: 'One particular night Paul and Mike decided we were going to have a barbecue on the beach there. We hunted up all the South African girls we could find and we went out to this beach in the middle of nowhere, and Paul again had a loan car from Ford in South Africa, and Mike had his Iso Grifo. Of course, they didn't think about the tide coming in! We were all extremely pissed, and consequently they had to leave them there. The following morning we all went back, and of course they wouldn't start because they'd all been flooded, and we had to drag them back off the beach. That was typical of what he always did.'

As far as Paul was concerned, the series was going just fine. He was out to enjoy life to the full, and only racing would otherwise focus his attention. Which is exactly what happened on Boxing Day at Pietmaritzburg, Natal. It would be a race fraught with difficulties. First Mike de Udy took the lead in

Paul's old Lola, only to develop problems that would blight his race, and the front running order was then 'Hawkeye', Piper and Hailwood, the latter soon overtaking them both to take the lead. Then it rained again. Everyone headed for the pits with the exception of Piper, who was playing it canny, which proved the right thing to do. The rain stopped, and David Piper was now two laps in front of the Mirage, with Paul in third.

At this point in the race, the lap counters threw a thrombi, and no-one was entirely certain of track position. Each team simply told their driver which car it was in front of them they had to beat. Paul was given the tall order to overtake the Hailwood Mirage once and Piper's Ferrari twice. Which is precisely what he did, charging through the field in superb sliding style. There would be a recount for second place, but it was a clear victory for the talented Aussie and his CanAm Ferrari yet again.

The final race of the series, at East London, would go down to the wire as Digby Martland's Porsche in the 2-litre class was on equal points with 'Hawkeye', and unless the big-banger CanAm car won outright there was a high probability that Martland would take the prize. Naturally, Paul was well aware of the potential for history to repeat itself following last year's escapade in the Lola, and he was determined as ever to fight to the last. To win the Championship he *had* to win the race.

He practised just under the lap record to put his Ferrari on the front of the grid, while Mike de Udy had a huge 150mph spin, damaging his Lola's bodywork, and Hailwood's Mirage chewed its gearbox into a few thousand pieces of useless chaff. David Piper was also having difficulty, but the following day he put his beautiful P4 second on the grid behind Paul in pre-race practice. Mike de Udy then turned up in the T70 without a nose fitted, did a few laps to assess the implications, and decided to chance the race.

Unsurprisingly, by the end of the first lap the order was 'Hawkeye', Piper, de Udy, and within a few laps David Piper had closed the gap on Paul, sitting inches behind in his slipstream.

This was a dangerous position for Paul, as David had won the Championship on numerous occasions, knew the track well, and represented a huge threat. As parts of the newly surfaced track began to break up, they were obliged to take particular care, and on lap 10 Paul's big Ferrari suddenly lost grip. David aimed the P4 for the gap, but Paul was having nothing of it, caught the slide and regained track position.

Unfortunately, David was occupying the space at that time, and the pair crunched expensively. As the CanAm car lost half its nose, the P4 suffered a freshly redesigned side panel, but the pair fought on, until David noticed that he was leaking fuel, which was a *slight* worry. He immediately headed for the pits, but didn't make it. The leaking fuel tank instantly ignited, and as he swung the car onto the grass to escape the searing flames there was no time to hit the extinguisher. Within seconds his car was reduced to nothing but a charred wreck, of which the only recognizable parts were the engine and gearbox.

Paul soldiered on in his freshly redesigned car, while behind him the field was being decimated. Now in second place, Mike de Udy's noseless Lola started behaving strangely. As he watched a front wheel moving sideways, he concluded that there might just be a small problem, the result of which had him spinning like a top at points all around the circuit. On one of these excursions Joubert's Chevron was forced to a halt behind him, where he was promptly speared by a following saloon, and both were out.

Mike's wandering minstrel show now began behaving not just strangely but very badly indeed as the chassis, in fact damaged in the previous day's accident, now split asunder, leaving the Lola sliding its nose along the ground. Unfortunately, this was not before he had also collected the Lucas Porsche 910, forcing it into the pits to drop a place. Shortly after, Serrurier's Lola ground to a halt with gearbox munchies, and suddenly Martland's 2-litre Porsche was in fourth place.

Though it was largely bodywork damage on Paul's car, it

nevertheless had the potential to affect its high-speed stability, and the ever increasing marbles of tarmac remained a perpetual problem. But as he crossed the finish line, the 10,000 strong crowd let rip, for 'Hawkeye' had at long last cornered the market in the Springbok series – albeit that the prize money would be shared with Martland, who had finished on equal points. And, of course, it was party time.

Yet again, Richie Bray was sitting in the passenger seat on the way home. 'He hadn't drunk a hell of a lot,' he maintains, and of course Paul was driving in his usual cautious and considerate manner. 'Going through the suburbs of Johannesburg, he slid off the road and hit a tree in someone's garden. It was a hire car, I think; hit a tree, spun it back around and flipped it back over. We were both quite badly cut on our backs because the screen had come in behind us, and I do remember Paul saying that we'd better get out of here and leg it in a hurry. We went back the following day, and we'd gone through this absolutely immaculate garden. Absolutely destroyed it.' Road car number three had now been written-off, and perhaps it was just as well that it was time to return to the remains of winter in blighty, where Jackie Epstein had been rather busy helping out Eric Broadley in his new role of works manager for Lola Cars.

Jackie and Paul had already decided they wanted to run a Lola for the coming '69 season, and they weren't the only ones who had come to that decision. Jackie: 'Eric wanted us to run one of these late cars, and we had a sponsor that we'd picked up at the Racing Car Show. This guy appeared on the stand one day and said that he liked the look of the car and he wanted to help us go racing. A guy called Nick Cuthbert. He was a motorsport enthusiast, and he'd never driven a racing car as far as I'm aware. He said: 'Yes, I'll buy the chassis and I'll put money into the team.'

Faced with that I went back to Eric and said: 'Right, we've got the funding to run a works team, either Paul will drive the car or, if he's off somewhere else, Mike Hailwood will drive it.' This was exactly what Paul was looking for, and on February 5th a brand spanking new, bright red (of course) Lola T70 Mk 3b Coupe, chassis SL76/142, was delivered to Nick Cuthbert for use by Paul Hawkins Racing Ltd, which now made the logical move from Fortis Green.

Jackie: 'My association with the Lola factory, in particular Eric Broadley, was getting stronger and stronger all the time, and Eric said: "Well, you'd better come and base down here." So he gave us a piece of the workshop, put up a wall, and we could run Paul Hawkins Racing, and anything else we wanted to run, out of the factory.'

The Lola would fall under the new(ish) CSI regulations, and with a 5-litre 450bhp Traco engine fitted, the developmental arm of Lola Cars was now in business running the Mk 3b under the Group 4 GT regulations for Paul, and a T42 for Mike Hailwood in the newly formed Formula 5000 series.

The pair were already firm friends before teaming up with Lola, and having originally met up in South Africa some five years earlier, they had more recently cemented that friendship on the beaches of Mozambique and the restaurants of Johannesburg. It was Mike who had also been offered Paul's open seat at JWA, sitting alongside David Hobbs, so there was much in common to talk about. However, it was perhaps a little surprising that the son of a preacher from the backblocks of suburban Australia should get on so well with the English son of a brash millionaire. While Paul had a reputation as a hell-raiser, Mike's was much more that of being motor racing's Mister Nice Guy. Perhaps it was a friendship of opposites, but the pair somehow gelled, and Paul would increasingly spend time at Mike's place down near the airport.

The team got down to business, and late in March tested in preparation for their Le Mans effort, setting a time of 3min 35.2sec, which was good enough for third fastest on the Sarthe circuit. The very next day was the new Lola's first outing at Silverstone, and a Group 4 third was a fair indicator of the car's potential. Here Paul bumped into Jose Juncadella, who had purchased his old GT40, and was experiencing some difficulty.

Paul typically offered his time and help, but unfortunately, on this occasion his generosity was just a little too exuberant, and he blew the Spaniard's engine in a rather big way before buying him a pint. Four days later, and a win at Snetterton confirmed their belief in the car, and following a third at Thruxton, Paul was feeling good and the future seemed assured.

Whilst the Lolas were undoubtedly fast, they had also developed a reputation for being fragile, and after a wishbone breakage at Brands Hatch in the prestigious BOAC 500, Paul headed for Italy, where his previous garage neighbour David Piper had entered his own Lola in the Monza 1000 Kilometres. Here they qualified 13th on the grid behind the usual bunch of faster Group 6 prototypes, and a gaggle of Lolas and other Group 4 cars.

The factory had been quick to learn from their mistake at Brands, and the four Mk 3bs entered had all had their rear wishbones boxed-in following the failure just two weeks earlier; a clear demonstration of how the team's new development facility was able to react quickly to need. It was an aspect that both Paul and Jackie Epstein had always appreciated within a smaller, less hierarchical environment, though on this occasion it made no difference as a broken hub would see the Piper car retire.

Paul's bright red Lola was next out at Magny-Cours, and though in the race he again took a second place on the podium, it was his indomitable party spirit (or spirit of another kind) that was once again to the fore, demonstrating convincingly that he wasn't about to change his naturally evolved, likeable and very colourful character.

Having made the move with him to Lola's trading estate address in Slough, Richie Bray well remembers this latest escapade in France: 'It was the night after the race, he'd had a fair bit to drink and he was out looking for a bit of fun. The town itself had a lovely big green in the middle of the shopping area, but in the middle of this area were all the corporation buses. We were all walking around the town and Paul says: "Jeezes, matey, I'm going to go and pinch one of those f***ing buses."

'Lo and behold, off he went. The stupid thing was, these buses had the keys in them! We all legged it down the road. We wanted nothing to do with this, and by the time we'd got to the nearest bar and ordered a beer, of course who comes driving by in one of these old-fashioned articulated bendy-buses? There's Paul and David Prophet in this bloody bendy-bus driving around Magny-Cours hitting cars! Eventually, I think, they crashed into something and they legged it. Everybody else said: "Look, we'd better get out of it because the police will know it's something to do with the racing," so we all legged it as well.'

Moving forward to May 1969, and the first *Apollo* mission to the moon was near. Paul took a fourth at Silverstone, where his throttle linkage stuck, and then it was on to Oulton Park, where he already held a pair of track records and happy memories of his *Autosport* Championship two years earlier. This time he would be driving the Lola in the Tourist Trophy race...

Years later, Paul's minister father would write to journalist Barry Green. 'At Oulton Park the day before he died, he went into a small Anglican church opposite the *Red Lion Hotel* in Little Budworth, where he was staying, and stayed there for almost two hours. We wonder if he had a premonition of an approaching confrontation with God, who awaits us at the end of the road of every man's life.'

While his father, Bill, was now proud of his son's achievements in his chosen career, he had barely seen him to talk to over the past decade, and would probably have appreciated more time to get to know the man he had become. 'I distinctly remember going into this church,' says Richie Bray. 'It was peeing down with rain, and there was nothing we could do, because in those days there were no covered pits or anything. There was Paul and I and (Paul's secretary) Norma. *It was just somewhere to walk around.*' It seems somehow sad to dismiss his father's dream, but that was the reality of Paul Hawkins. His upbringing had long ago forged a complete rejection of any religious hopes his father may have had for him, whilst motor racing and its inherent risk had meanwhile tempered his capacity for enjoying life into a rough and ready art form. He had lived his life to the limit; whether it was on or off the race track, and his effervescent character and outrageous humour had by now enshrined his memory as an integral part of motor racing history.

Back at the circuit on that wet afternoon, Paul was helping out his protégé Chris Skeaping, offering pit crew support to his Chevron. Paul was on a roll. His Lola – whilst fragile – had potential, he was talking about buying a Lamborghini, and was thinking about how to set up a full-bore Lola sports car team for the following year, planning to become his own team manager. Life was good, and there was still a lot of fun to be had.

That night, a big marquee reception had been arranged by the race organizers in the grounds of a nearby stately joint. Unwisely, they had neglected to invite several of their members, amongst whom were Chris and Paul. This represented social high handedness and snobbery of unacceptable proportions as far as Paul was concerned, and his lifelong dislike of authority figures, jobsworth types and pomposity overflowed.

'Matey, some fun here,' he might have said in his usual gruff tones, as Chris remembers: 'We went anyway. Paul organized that we let down all the tents around the occupants inside.' And whilst the good and glamorous regretted their choice of select company as they staggered, blundered and swore in the darkness of the collapsed canvas, he went one further, as he always did – and dropped the tents on top of those still sitting on the toilet seats!'

It was 'Hawkeye' at his outrageous best. And still they would forgive him.

'When we went to his funeral in London – quite a few of us went along, because it was Paul – and we said: "We're not going to wear black ties for Paul Hawkins." And we went with coloured ties. For Him. Because he would have said: "Hey, come on, don't be bloody miserable. I've gone. Enjoy yourself...".'

Vic Elford

Appendix One

Just a thought...

'Paul was my educator in life...I went out (to South Africa) drinking milk as a 22-year-old and came back drinking beer.'
Mike Brown

'He lived very hard. He played very hard. And of course he drove very hard.'
Richie Bray

'His character was etched on his face.'
Spike Winter

'I still remember the old bugger with great affection.'
Ken Brittain

'I could always trust Paul Hawkins. He was a genuine guy.'
Christabel Carlisle

'He was a bloody good driver. He would drive anything, anywhere. He was a great professional.'
Chris Skeaping

'He was a rough diamond (in the nicest possible way).'
Jack Sears

'He was quite a character. He would call a spade a spade, and couldn't care a Continental who thought what about it.'
Bob Olthoff

'Paul was a great team-mate, great competitor, and a lot of fun. He was one of the great privateer owner-drivers.'
Brian Redman

'The only advantage I had was that some people are runners, and some people are screamers; I'm a screaming runner and he could never catch me. Otherwise I would have been in for a real tricky time.'
Mike Brown

'He inevitably got into all sorts of strife. He wouldn't do it deliberately, but he automatically got into trouble.'
Jackie Epstein

'He introduced me to the 'golden nectar' early on in the piece and I am still drinking it today.'
Ian Walker

'Any experience with Paul was pretty wild. He was a colourful character.'
David Piper

'Paul was Paul, and there was only one mould that would have housed Paul Hawkins, I can assure you.'
Frank Gardner

'He was a smashing bloke who never gave up.'
Cyril Simson

'I am sure that Paul would have gone on to be a major influence in motor sport, and the world is a poorer place with the loss of people like him, who are becoming increasingly rare.'
Peter Jackson

'He was here to enjoy himself. Anywhere, to enjoy himself.'
John Etheridge

'You just feel you were robbed.'
John Etheridge's mum

'He enjoyed life. He was very straight-forward, no pomposity, and if he didn't like you he'd tell you. He wouldn't pretend otherwise. Just a completely straight-forward, honest guy.'
Vic Elford

'Just a real lively, bubbly, typical Aussie. He'd got all the sayings and the repartee.'
John Pledger

'He was a great character. He was a great driver as well.'
David Baker

'On race weekend he had a big sense of humour. We had fun. He was joking, and when he was sending darts they were very accurate; to the point.'
Jacky Ickx

'He was a very amusing person to have around. Never a dull moment. On the track he was a good driver.'
John Horsman

'I just guess he sort of thought "kind of my way or the highway", and in lots of things in life that's fine.'
David Hobbs

'He was a first-class driver. If it came to long-distance racing, I wouldn't hesitate to put him in any car. He could drive fast and conservatively.'
Steele Therkleson

'Paul was larger than life as well as being a very accomplished driver, and an extremely likeable man. He is sorely missed, and one of life's highly amusing characters who could keep all and sundry in fits of laughter.'
Paddy Driver

Appendix Two

Paul Hawkins'
racing record

Although it is known that Paul entered races other than those listed, the following record is as complete and accurate as can be ascertained. Where records have conflicted every effort has been made to ensure accuracy.

DATE and CIRCUIT	EVENT and RESULT	CAR and CO-DRIVER(S)	COMMENTS

1958

DATE and CIRCUIT	EVENT and RESULT	CAR and CO-DRIVER(S)	COMMENTS
March – Phillip Island (AUS)	Sports car race – class 1st	Austin-Healey 100S	PH's first circuit race
Nov 30 – Albert Park (AUS)	Sports car scratch race – 5th	Austin-Healey 100S	Entered by F. Agostino & Co

1960

DATE and CIRCUIT	EVENT and RESULT	CAR and CO-DRIVER(S)	COMMENTS
April 30 – Aintree (GB)	Aintree 200 support race – class 1st	Team 221 Austin-Healey Sprite	Class fastest lap 70.68mph
May 22 – Nürburgring (D)	ADAC 1000 Kms – class 6th	Austin-Healey Sprite S221 – PH/Cyril Simson	
June 12 – Rouen les Essarts (F)	Grand Prix de Rouen – DNF	Austin-Healey Sprite – PH/Cyril Simson	
Aug 20 – Goodwood (GB)	RAC Tourist Trophy – 20th, class 7th	Austin-Healey Sprite S221	Car no 50 transferred to 1300-2000cc class
Sept 4 – Nürburgring (D)	ADAC 500 Kms – class 1st	Austin-Healey Sprite S221	
Nov 21-26 – (GB)	RAC Rally – 37th, class 4th	Austin-Healey Sprinzel Sprite 2214 UE – PH/John Patten	Iris Blue
Dec 26 – Brands Hatch (GB)	Unlimited GT race	Austin-Healey Sprite 2214 UE	Arrived too late for GT race

DATE and CIRCUIT	EVENT and RESULT	CAR and CO-DRIVER(S)	COMMENTS

1961

DATE and CIRCUIT	EVENT and RESULT	CAR and CO-DRIVER(S)	COMMENTS
Mar 24 – Sebring (USA)	4 Hours GT race – class 7th	Austin-Healey Sebring Sprite – PH/Pat Moss	Originally to drive PMO 200
Mar 25 – Sebring (USA)	12 Hours – 37th, class 4th	Austin-Healey Sprite – PH/Cyril Simson	
May 28 – Nürburgring (D)	ADAC 1000 Kms – DNF	Austin-Healey Sebring Sprite – PH/Cyril Simson	
June 3 – Brands Hatch (GB)	Peco Trophy – class 3rd	Austin-Healey Sebring Sprite S221	
June 10/11 – Le Mans (F)	24 Hours – 40th	Austin-Healey Super Sprite – PH/John Colgate	Donald Healey works entry, formerly 8426 UE
July 8 – Silverstone (GB)	Peco Trophy – class 3rd	Austin-Healey Sprite S221	First best practice lap
Aug 7 – Silverstone (GB)	Peco Trophy – class 3rd	Austin-Healey Sprite PMO 200	
Aug 12 – Silverstone (GB)	750MC Relay race – team 1st	Austin-Healey Sprite PMO 200	Car no 21A
Sept 3 – Nürburgring (D)	500 Kms – 7th	Austin-Healey Sprite D 20 – PH/Ian Walker	Manufacturers' team prize
Nov 13-18 – (GB)	RAC Rally – DNF	Austin-Healey Sprite PMO 200 – PH/Vic Elford	Rear springs and gearbox failure

1962

DATE and CIRCUIT	EVENT and RESULT	CAR and CO-DRIVER(S)	COMMENTS
April 7 – Oulton Park (GB)	BARC meeting – 4th, class 1st	Lotus-Ford 23/1098cc	Ian Walker Racing
April 23 – Goodwood (GB)	BARC meeting – class 1st	Lotus-Ford 23/1098cc	Up to 1500cc class
April 28 – Aintree (GB)	Event 1 – DNF	Lotus-Ford 23/1098cc	
May 12 – Silverstone (GB)	12-lap sports car race – 7th	Lotus-Ford 23/1098cc	
May 28 – Nürburgring (D)	ADAC 1000 Kms – DNF	Lotus-Ford 23/1098cc – PH/Peter Ryan	Class lap record 10:26.6
June 11 – Crystal Palace (GB)	10-lap sports car race – 1st	Lotus-Ford 23/1098cc	Class lap record 1:1.8
June 24 – Monza (I)	Lottery GP FJ race – Heat 1 2nd, Final 3rd	Lotus-Ford 22 FJ	
July 15 – Clermont-Ferrand (F)	Sports car race – 22nd	Lotus-Ford 23/1500cc	Fastest practice lap, gearbox failure
Aug 6 – Brands Hatch (GB)	50-lap sports car race – 2nd	Lotus-Ford 23/1500cc	Class fastest lap
Aug 26 – Roskilde (DK)	Copenhagen GP meeting – 3rd	Lotus-Ford 22 FJ	
Aug 26 – Roskilde (DK)	Copenhagen GP meeting – 1st	Lotus-Ford 23	1st overall and lap record
Sept 1 – Oulton Park (GB)	Gold Cup meeting – DNF	Lotus-Ford 23	6th on grid, retired clutch
Sept 9 – Languedoc (F)	Heat 1 – DNF	Lotus-Ford 22 FJ	

1963

DATE and CIRCUIT	EVENT and RESULT	CAR and CO-DRIVER(S)	COMMENTS
April 6 – Oulton Park (GB)	Formula Junior – 3rd	Brabham-Ford BT6/1100cc	Car no 92 scratched from sports car race
April 11 – Goodwood (GB)	Chichester Cup – 4th	Brabham-Ford BT6/1100cc	Car no 10/114??
April 27 – Aintree (GB)	Aintree 200 – DNF	Brabham-Ford BT6 FJ	No 38, accident lap 10
April 27 – Aintree (GB)	Sports cars to 1150cc – 2nd	Lotus-Ford 23	Car no 89
May 11 – Silverstone (GB)	BRDC meeting – 3rd	Brabham-Ford BT6 FJ	Car no 5
May 11 – Silverstone (GB)	Sports car race – class 1st	Lotus-Ford 23	
May 19 – Montlhéry (F)	Heat 1 – DNF	Brabham-Ford BT6 FJ	No 26, accident, locked brake
May 25 – Monaco (F)	FJ race – DNS	Brabham-Ford BT6	
June 2 – Mallory Park (GB)	FJ race – 3rd/4th?	Brabham-Ford BT6	Car no 21
June 3 – Crystal Palace (GB)	Anerley Trophy Heat 1 5th, Heat 2 DNF	Brabham-Ford BT6 FJ	Car no 26, accident, lost brakes on lap 19
June 23 – Rouen les Essarts (F)	FJ race – Heat 1 2nd, Final 1st	Brabham-Ford BT6	Car no 16, average 98.98mph
June 30 – Reims (F)	25-lap sports & GT race – 5th	Lotus-Ford 23B T/C	
June 30 – Reims (F)	FJ race – DNF	Brabham-Ford BT6	Car no 18, retired lap 12
July 7 – Clermont-Ferrand (F)	FJ race – Heat 1 6th, Heat 2 DNF	Brabham-Ford BT6	Classified 14th overall
July 13 – Mallory Park (GB)	Guards Trophy meeting – Heat 2 3rd, Final 4th	Lotus-Ford 23	
July 20 – Silverstone (GB)	FJ race – DNF	Brabham-Ford BT6	Broken suspension lap 2
July 20 – Silverstone (GB)	25-lap sports & GT race – class 1st	Lotus-Ford 23B	Class fastest lap
July 28 – Solitude (D)	FJ race – 7th	Brabham-Ford BT6	Car no 36
Aug 4 – Brands Hatch (GB)	Sports car race – unplaced	Lotus-Ford 23B	
August 24 – Goodwood (GB)	FJ race – 7th	Brabham-Ford BT6	Car no 18
August 25 – Zolder (B)	FJ race – 4th	Brabham-Ford BT6	Seized wheel bearing
Sept 1 – Zandvoort (NL)	FJ race – 5th	Brabham-Ford BT6	
Sept 8 – Albi (F)	FJ race – Heat 1 4th, Heat 2 5th	Brabham-Ford BT6	Car no 7
Sept 14 – Brands Hatch (GB)	FJ race – Heat 1 6th, Final 6th	Brabham-Ford BT6	Car no 33
Sept 21 – Oulton Park (GB)	Sports car race – 8th, class 1st	Lotus-Ford 23B	Class fastest lap 1:48.8
Sept 28 – Snetterton (GB)	Sports cars 1150cc – 1st	Lotus-Ford 23B	
Nov 2 – Kyalami (SA)	Rand 9 Hours – DNF	Ford Galaxie – PH/Jack Sears	Willment entry
Dec 1 – James McNiellie (RHO)	Production cars – 2nd	Ford Lotus Cortina	Willment entry
Dec 1 – James McNiellie (RHO)	Production cars unlimited – 2nd	Ford Lotus Cortina	Willment entry
Dec 14 – Kyalami (SA)	Rand GP – 1st	AC Cobra	Willment entry, Rand GP meeting
Dec 28 – East London (SA)	S. African GP meeting – 3rd	Ford Galaxie	Willment entry

1964

DATE and CIRCUIT	EVENT and RESULT	CAR and CO-DRIVER(S)	COMMENTS
Jan 4 – Killarney (SA)	Saloon cars – Heat 1 2nd, Heat 2 3rd	Ford Galaxie	
April 5 – Pau (F)	F2 race – 7th	Alexis-Cosworth Mk 4	Car borrowed from Bill Harris
April 12 – Aspern (A)	F2 race – Heat 1 DNF, Heat 2 9th, overall 10th	Alexis-Cosworth Mk 4	No 22
April 26 – Nürburgring (D)	Eifelrennen F2 race – 6th	Alexis-Cosworth Mk 4	Team Alexis Car no 8
May 2 – Silverstone (GB)	International Trophy – class 2nd	Lotus-Ford 23	Willment
May 7 – Monza (I)	F2 race – 12th	Alexis-Cosworth Mk 4	Willment
May 18 – Crystal Palace (GB)	Anerley Trophy – 4th	Lotus-Ford 23/1098cc	Willment car no 31
May 31 – Nürburgring (D)	ADAC 1000 Kms – class 3rd	AC Cobra – PH/Olthoff	Cars over 3000cc
June 6 – Brands Hatch (GB)	Touring cars – DNF	Ford Cortina GT	Willment
June 13 – Crystal Palace (GB)	Sports cars – class 4th	Lotus-Ford 23	Willment
July 11 – Brands Hatch (GB)	Guards Trophy – 11th	Lotus-Ford 23	Willment
July 19 – Snetterton (GB)	Sports cars – class 2nd	Lotus-Ford 23	Fastest lap 1:46.8
July 25 – Aintree (GB)	Sports cars – DNF	Lotus-Ford 23/1098cc	Car no 4, fastest lap 1:12.0
Aug 3 – Brands Hatch (GB)	British Eagle F2 Trophy – 16th	Lola-Cosworth T55	Car no 60
Aug 9 – Pergusa (I)	F2 race – Heat 1 2nd, Final 3rd	Lola-Cosworth T55	Shared fastest lap 1:22.1, Willment car no 24
Aug 16 – Pergusa (I)	Mediterranean GP – DNF	Lola-Cosworth T55 1500cc	10th on grid, Willment
Aug 23 – Zolder (B)	Limburg GP – Heat 1 DNF	Lola-Cosworth T55	Willment
Sept 5/6? – Crystal Palace (GB)	Sports-racing 1150cc – 6th	Lotus-Ford 23	Willment
Sept 13 – Albi (F)	F2 race – 4th	Lola-Cosworth T55	Willment
Sept 19 – Oulton Park (GB)	Gold Cup F2 – 5th	Lola-Cosworth T55 Mk 5A	Car no 22
Sept 26 – Snetterton (GB)	Vanwall Trophy F2 – 6th	Lola-Cosworth T55	Willment
Oct 26/27 – Snetterton (GB)	F2/F3 race – 6th	Lola-Cosworth T55	Willment
Oct 26/27 – Snetterton (GB)	Autosport 3 Hours – 18th	Lotus-Ford 23	
Nov 29 – James McNiellie (RHO)	Rhodesian GP – 1st	Brabham-Cosworth BT10	Fastest lap
Nov 29 – James McNiellie (RHO)	Saloon car race – 1st	Ford Galaxie	Class record
Dec 12 – Kyalami (SA)	Rand GP – Heat 1 3rd, Heat 2 2nd, overall 2nd	Brabham-Ford BT10 1.5ltr	No 4, Willment entry. Chassis F2–4–64
Dec 12 – Kyalami (SA)	Saloons – 1st	Ford Galaxie	Fastest lap

DATE and CIRCUIT	EVENT and RESULT	CAR and CO-DRIVER(S)	COMMENTS

1965

DATE and CIRCUIT	EVENT and RESULT	CAR and CO-DRIVER(S)	COMMENTS
Jan 1 – East London (SA)	South African GP – 9th	Brabham-Ford BT10	No 18, chassis F2–4-64, Willment entry
Jan 9 – East London (SA)	South Easter Trophy – 1st	Brabham-Ford 1600cc	
Mar 13 –Brands Hatch (GB)	Race of Champions – Heat 2 DNF	Lotus-Climax 33	No 25, classified 10th
Mar 20 – Silverstone (GB)	F2 race – DNS	Alexis-Cosworth 997cc	No 30, race abandoned – weather
Mar 27 – Sebring (USA)	12 Hours – class 1st	Austin-Healey 3000 – PH/Warwick Banks	Class GT12
April 3 – Oulton Park (GB)	F2 race – DNF	Alexis-Cosworth SCA	Team Alexis
April 19 – Goodwood (GB)	International Trophy – DNF	Lotus-Climax 33	Car no 15
April 25 – Nürburgring (D)	Eifelrennen F2 – 1st	Alexis-Cosworth Mk 6	South circuit used. Team Alexis
May 9 – Madonie, Sicily (I)	Targa Florio – class 2nd	Austin-Healey 3000 – PH/Timo Makinen	Broken rotor arm delayed car when leading GT2000-3000 class
May 15 – Silverstone (GB)	International Trophy – 10th	Lotus-Climax 33 R8	Started row 5
May 23 – Nürburgring (D)	ADAC 1000 Kms – DNF	Porsche 904 – PH/Mike de Udy	
May 30 – Monaco (MC)	Monaco GP – DNF	Lotus-Climax 33	No 10, plunged into harbour on lap 80 when running 9th
June 9/10 – Le Mans (F)	24 Hours – class 1st	Austin-Healey Super Sprite ENX 414C – PH/John Rhodes	12th overall and 1st 1300cc class
July 3 – Reims (F)	Reims 12 Hours – 6th	Porsche 904 – PH/Mike de Udy	
July 3 – Reims (F)	F2 race – 11th	Lola-Cosworth T55	Midland Racing Partnership entry
July 11 – Rouen les Essarts (F)	F2 race – 8th	Lola-Cosworth T55	MRP entry, car no 34
July 18 – Solitude (D)	F2 race – DNF	Lola-BRM T60	Car no 34, low oil pressure
Aug 1 – Nürburgring (D)	German GP – DNF	Lotus-Climax 33	DW Racing, car no 22, oil leak
Aug 8 – Karlskoga (S)	Canon F2 race – 6th	Lola-Cosworth T55	MRP entry, old car, lapped 1:27.6
Aug 11 – Rouen les Essarts (F)	F2 Champ race – 8th	Lola-Cosworth T55	MRP entry, lapped 2:25.8
Aug 15 – Marlboro (USA)	12 Hours – 2nd	Ford Lotus Cortina – PH/Roy Pierpoint	English Ford Line Operations
Sept 18 – Oulton Park (GB)	F2 Gold Cup – 9th	Lola-Cosworth T60	MRP entry
Sept 26 – Albi (F)	F2 race – DNF	Lola-Cosworth T60	MRP entry, puncture
Nov 6 – Kyalami (SA)	9 Hours – 3rd	Ferrari 250LM 0 PH/Jackie Epstein	First drive with Epstein
Nov 28 – James McNiellie (RH)	Sports cars – 1st	Lola-Ford T70	David Good's car
Dec 4 – Kyalami (SA)	Rand GP – 3rd	Lotus-Climax 25 2.7ltr R3	Parnell car
Dec 4 – Kyalami (SA)	20-lap sports cars – DNF	Lola-Ford T70	David Good 's car
Dec 27 – Roy Hesketh (SA)	3 Hours – DNF	Lola-Ford T70	Holed piston

1966

DATE and CIRCUIT	EVENT and RESULT	CAR and CO-DRIVER(S)	COMMENTS
Jan 1 – East London (SA)	South African GP – DNF	Lotus-Climax 33 2.7ltr	Parnell car, broken selector
Jan 8 – Killarney (SA)	Cape S. Easter Trophy – Heat 1 3rd, Heat 2 DNS	Lotus-Climax 33	Parnell car, fastest lap
Feb 5/6 – Daytona (USA)	24 Hours – DNF	Ferrari 250LM – PH/Jackie Epstein	
Mar 26 – Sebring (USA)	12 Hours – class 1st, 18th overall	Austin-Healey Super Sprite – PH/Timo Makinen	Entered by Donald Healey
April 2/3 – Le Mans (F)	Le Mans trials	AMGT-2	PH later bought this car
May 1 – Syracuse (I)	Syracuse GP – DNF	Lotus-Climax 25 2.7ltr	Parnell car
May 8 – Madonie, Sicily (I)	Targa Florio – Sports/GT cars – 24th	Ferrari 275LM – PH/Jackie Epstein	Tyre difficulties
May 14 – Silverstone (GB)	International Trophy – 8th	Lotus-Climax 33 2.7ltr	Parnell car
May 22 – Spa-Francorchamps (B)	1000 Kms – 7th	Ferrari 275LM – PH/Jackie Epstein	Epstein car
May 30 – Crystal Palace (GB)	Saloon race – class 2nd, 6th overall	Ford Lotus Cortina	Willment car
June 5 – Nürburgring (D)	1000 Kms – 4th	Porsche 906 Carrera – PH/Bob Bondurant	Porsche factory drive
June 18/19 – Le Mans (F)	24 Hours – DNF	Ford GT40 Mk 2 7ltr – PH/Mark Donohue	Retired, broken differential, 7.29pm
July 10 – Rouen les Essarts (F)	Rouen GP – DNF	Lola-Cosworth T60	MRP car, failed doughnut, lap 12
Aug 21 – Surfers Paradise (AUS)	12 Hours – class 3rd, 5th overall	Ferrari 275LM – PH/Jackie Epstein	John Hawkins as pit crew
Aug 29 – Brands Hatch (GB)	Guards Trophy – Heat 1 6th, Heat 26th, 5th overall	Lola-Chevrolet T70	First outing of Jackie Epstein's CanAm car SL71/38
Sept 11 – St Jovite (CAN)	CanAm – DNS	Lola-Chevrolet T70	Car crashed in practice
Sept 18 – Bridgehampton (USA)	CanAm – 15th	Lola-Chevrolet T70	Car no 25 now in primer
Sept 25 – Mosport (CAN)	CanAm – 5th	Lola-Chevrolet T70	Car no 11, 5 points
Oct 9 – Pacific Raceway (USA)	North West GP – 3rd	Lola-Chevrolet T70	
Oct 16 – Laguna Seca (USA)	CanAm – Heat 1 DNF, Heat 2 14th	Lola-Chevrolet T70	
Oct 30 – Riverside (USA)	CanAm – 7th	Lola-Chevrolet T70	
Nov 13 – Las Vegas (USA)	CanAm – 8th	Lola-Chevrolet T70	

DATE and CIRCUIT	EVENT and RESULT	CAR and CO-DRIVER(S)	COMMENTS

1967

DATE and CIRCUIT	EVENT and RESULT	CAR and CO-DRIVER(S)	COMMENTS
Mar 24 – Snetterton (GB)	*Autosport* Trophy Gp4 sports cars – 1st	Ford GT40 AMGT2	Car no 52, first outing
Mar 27 – Silverstone (GB)	Gp4 sports cars – 2nd	Ford GT40 AMGT2	Car no 4, car blue
April 29 – Silverstone (GB)	WD&HO Wills Trophy – 3rd	Ford GT40 AMGT2	Car no 29
May 1 – Spa-Francorchamps (B)	1000 Kms – 4th	Lola T70 coupe SL73/112 – PH/Jackie Epstein	First outing for new Epstein coupe
May 14 – Madonie, Sicily (I)	Targa Florio – 1st	Porsche 910/8 – PH/Rolf Stommelen	Factory entry
May 20 – Silverstone (GB)	Martini Trophy – 1st	Ford GT40 AMGT2	Car no 44 in primer
May 20 – Silverstone (GB)	Saloon cars – 4th	Ford Lotus Cortina	Replacement for Graham Hill
May 28 – Nürburgring (D)	ADAC 1000 Kms – 2nd	Porsche 910/6 – PH/Gerhard Koch	Factory entry
May 29 – Crystal Palace (GB)	Norbury Trophy – 1st	Ford GT40 AMGT2	Car no 42, now repainted red
May 29 – Crystal Palace (GB)	Gp6 race – DNF	Lola T70 SL73/112 – PH/Jackie Epstein	Clutch failure
June 10/11 – Le Mans (F)	24 Hours – DNF	Ford GT40 Mk2B – PH/Ronnie Bucknum	Retired, engine failure, 9.40am
June 18 – Clermont-Ferrand (F)	Auvergne Trophy – 1st	Ford GT40 AMGT2	Practice accident
June 24/25 – Reims (F)	12 Hours – DNF	Lola T70 SL73/112 – PH/Jackie Epstein	Broken bellhousing. Fitted with extra-high 4th gear, outright lap record 236km/h
July 2 – Norisring (D)	Gp4 race – Heat 1 2nd, Heat 2 DNF	Ford GT40 AMGT2	Pipe detached from gearbox oil cooler
July 15 – Silverstone (GB)	Gp4 race – DNF	Ford GT40 AMGT2	Holed piston when leading, new class record 1:46
July 15 – Silverstone (GB)	Saloon race – class 1st, 4th overall	Ford Lotus Cortina Mk2	
July 30 – Brands Hatch (GB)	BOAC 6 Hours – 6th	Ferrari 330 P4 – PH/Jonathan Williams	Factory entry, lost rear bodywork when in 3rd place
Aug 13 – Karlskoga (S)	Gp4 race – DNF	Ford GT40 AMGT2	Worn camshaft lobes
Aug 20 – Zeltweg (A)	Austrian GP – 1st	Ford GT40 AMGT2	Engine rebuilt since Karlskoga, gearbox kills bearing
Aug 28 – Brands Hatch (GB)	Guards Trophy – 2nd	Ford GT40 AMGT2	New lap record despite only top two gears available
Sept 3 – Surfers Paradise (AUS)	12 Hours – 2nd	Lola-Chevrolet T70 Mk2 SL73/112 – PH/Jackie Epstein	Paul bought car from Jackie
Sept 16 – Oulton Park (GB)	Gold Cup meeting – 1st	Ford GT40 AMGT2	Won *Autosport* Championship and set new lap record of 1:39.8 on seven cylinders
Sept 24 – Skarpnack (S)	Gp4/6 race – 2nd	JWA Mirage M10003	Try-out weekend for JWA
Sept XX – Warwick Farm (AUS)	Gallagher GT Trophy – 1st	Lola T70 SL73/112	
Oct 1 – Bathurst (AUS)	Bathurst 1000 – class 5th	Alfa Romeo 1750	Stone holed radiator when leading
Oct 15 – Montlhéry (F)	Paris 1000 Kms – 1st	JWA Mirage 5.7ltr – PH/Jacky Ickx	First full drive for Gulf JWA team
Nov 4 – Kyalami (SA)	Kyalami 9 Hours – 2nd	Lola-Chevrolet 5.9ltr T70 SL73/112 – PH/John Love	
Nov 18 – Cape Town (SA)	Continental 3 Hours – 1st	Lola T70 SL73/112	
Dec 3 – Kumalo (RHO)	Gp6 race – DNF	Lola-Chevrolet T70 SL73/112	Cotton wool found in oil tank
Dec 3 – Kumalo (RHO)	Rhodesian GP – DNF	Cooper-Climax 2.7ltr	John Love's car, overheating
Dec 16 – Laurenco Marques (Port. E Africa)	3 Hours – 1st	Lola-Chevrolet T70 SL73/112	
Dec 26 – Roy Hesketh (SA)	3 Hours – 2nd	Lola-Chevrolet T70 SL73/112	Did not cross finish line

1967 lap records
Snetterton – Ford GT40 – 1:33.8 – 104.01mph – Gp4 sports cars
Crystal Palace – Ford GT40 – 55.6 – 90mph – Gp4 sports cars, shared with Mike Parkes' Ferrari 250LM
Oulton Park – Ford GT40 – 1:39.8 – 99.6mph – Gp4 sports cars
Silverstone GP circuit – Ford Lotus Cortina – 1:46 – 99.4mph – Gp5 saloons 1301-2000cc

1968

DATE and CIRCUIT	EVENT and RESULT	CAR and CO-DRIVER(S)	COMMENTS
Jan 6 – Killarney (SA)	South Easter meeting – Heat 1 1st, Heat 2 1st	Lola T70 SL73/112	
Feb 3 /4 – Daytona (USA)	24 Hours – DNF	Ford GT40 1074 – PH/David Hobbs	Fractured fuel tank
Mar 23 – Sebring (USA)	12 Hours – DNF	Ford GT40 1074 – PH/David Hobbs	Accident damage
April 7 – Brands Hatch (GB)	BOAC 6 Hours – 4th	Ford GT40 AMGT2 – PH/David Hobbs	Qualifier for Gp4 Championship
April 12 – Oulton Park (GB)	Spring Cup – 2nd	Ford GT40 AMGT2	Gp4 Autosport Championship
April 25 – Monza (I)	Monza 1000 Kms – 1st	Ford GT40 1074 – PH/David Hobbs	
April 27 – Silverstone (GB)	Players Trophy – 3rd	Ford GT40 1074 – PH/David Hobbs	Car suffering oil surge
May 12 – Zandvoort (NL)	Trophy of the Dunes – 1st	Ford GT40 AMGT2	PH Racing second car placed 3rd driven by Eric Liddell
May 19 – Nürburgring (D)	ADAC 1000 Kms – 3rd	Ford GT40 1074 – PH/Jacky Ickx	John Wyer switched drivers
May 26 – Spa-Francorchamps (B)	Spa 1000 Kms – 4th	Ford GT40 1084 – PH/David Hobbs	Falling oil pressure and failing brakes
June 3 – Oulton Park (GB)	RAC Tourist Trophy – 3rd	Ford GT40 AMGT2	Qualifier for Gp4 Championship
June 18 – Anderstorp (S)	Gp4/6 race – 2nd	Ford GT40 AMGT2	Eric Liddell 4th in other PH Racing entry
June 23 – Mallory Park (GB)	Guards International – 2nd	Ford GT40 AMGT2	Eric Liddell 4th in other PH racing entry
June 30 – Norisring (D)	Nurnburg 200 Miles – DNF	Ford GT40 AMGT2	Water pump bypass hose
July 7 – Vila Real (E)	Gp4/6 race – 3rd	Ford GT40 AMGT2	Eric Liddell 7th in 1019
July 14 – Watkins Glen (USA)	6 Hours – 2nd	Ford GT40 1074 – PH/David Hobbs	Paul eggs on David behind pits, contradicting pit signals
July 21 – Hockenheim (D)	20-lap sports cars – 3rd	Ford GT40 AMGT2	Borrows engine from Wyer
July 27 – Silverstone (GB)	Martini Trophy – 2nd	Ford GT40 AMGT2	No 5, qualifier for Gp4 Championship
Aug 11 – Karlskoga (S)	Swedish GP – 3rd	Ford GT40 AMGT2	Car no 1
Aug 17 – Oulton Park (GB)	*Speedworld Intl* – 3rd	Lola-Chevrolet T70	Car no 46, borrowed from Ulf Norinder
Aug 25 – Zeltweg (A)	Austrian GP – Gp4 1st, overall 3rd	Ford GT40 AMGT2	Car no 20
Sept 3 – Brands Hatch (GB)	Guards Trophy – 10th	Ford GT40 AMGT2	Puncture, lost Championship
Sept 15 – Hockenheim (D)	Gp4 race – 3rd	Ford GT40 AMGT2	
Sept 22 – Nürburgring (D)	Gp4 race – 1st	Ford GT40 AMGT2	Last race before being sold
Sept 29 – Le Mans (F)	24 Hours – DNF	Ford GT40 1074 – PH/David Hobbs	Clutch
Oct 6 – Bathurst (AUS)	Bathurst 1000 – DNF	Holden Monaro 327 – PH/Bill Brown	
Nov 23 – Kyalami (SA)	Rand 9 Hours – 3rd	Ferrari 330P4 0858	Hawkins Team 'G'
Dec 1 – Bulawayo (RHO)	15-lap Rhodesian GP – 2nd	Ferrari 330P4 0858	Hawkins Team 'G'
Dec 1 – Bulawayo (RHO)	25-lap sports cars – 1st	Ferrari 330P4 0858	Hawkins Team 'G
Dec 8 – Laurenco Marques (Port. E.Africa)	3 Hours – 2nd	Ferrari 330P4 0858	Hawkins Team 'G'
Dec 26 – Roy Hesketh (SA)	3 Hours – 1st	Ferrari 330P4 0858	Hawkins Team 'G'

1969

DATE and CIRCUIT	EVENT and RESULT	CAR and CO-DRIVER(S)	COMMENTS
Jan 4 – East London (SA)	500 Kms – 1st	Ferrari 330P4 0858	
Mar 30 – Silverstone (GB)	International Trophy Gp4 – 3rd	Lola-Chevrolet T70Mk3B	New car, chassis SL76/142
April 4 – Snetterton (GB)	Guards Trophy – 1st	Lola-Chevrolet T70Mk3B	Championship round 2
April 7 – Thruxton (GB)	Sports cars – 3rd	Lola-Chevrolet T70Mk3B	Championship round 3
April 13 – Brands Hatch (GB)	BOAC 500 – DNF	Lola-Chevrolet T70Mk3B	Broken wishbone
April 25 – Monza (I)	1000 Kms – DNF	Lola-Chevrolet T70Mk3B – PH/David Prophet	David Piper's car SL76/150
May 1 – Magny-Cours (F)	Sports cars – 2nd	Lola-Chevrolet T70Mk3B	SL76/142
May 11 – Spa-Francorchamps (B)	Sports cars – 8th	Lola-Chevrolet T70Mk3B	Engine failure after running 4th
May 17 – Silverstone (GB)	Martini International – 4th	Lola-Chevrolet T70Mk3B	Throttle linkage problem when leading
May 26 – Oulton Park	RAC Tourist Trophy – 7th	Lola-Chevrolet T70Mk3B	Fatal accident, race stopped

Bibliography

Books

CAN-AM – Pete Lyons – Motorbooks International

Formula 1 Register Record Book 1966 – Paul Sheldon with Duncan Rabagliati and Yves de la Gorce – St Leonards Press, Bradford

GT40: An Individual History and Race Record – Ronnie Spain – Osprey

Le Mans – Anders Ditlev Clausager – Arthur Barker, London

Lola T70 V8 Coupes: A Technical Appraisal – Ian Bamsey – Haynes

Lola T70: The Racing History and Individual Chassis Record (revised edn) – John Starkey – Veloce Publishing

Lotus: The Sports Racing Cars – Anthony Pritchard – Patrick Stephens

Men at the Wheel – Peter Miller – B.T. Batsford, London

Mighty Midgets & Special Sprites – John Baggott – The Crowood Press

Porsche – Anthony Pritchard – Pelham Books

Sports Car Championship – Anthony Pritchard – Robert Hale, London

Spritely Years – John Sprinzel and Tom Coulthard – Patrick Stephens

Sun on the Grid – Ken Stewart and Norman Reich – Hugh Keartland, Johannesburg

Targa Florio: 'The Porsche Years' 1965–1973 – Compiled by R.M. Clarke – Brooklands Books

The Certain Sound – John Wyer – Edita

The Formula One Record Book – John Thompson with Duncan

Rabagliati and Dr K Paul Sheldon – Leslie Frewin

The Ford That Beat Ferrari: A Racing History of the GT40 – Gordon Jones and John Allen – Motorbooks International

The Guinness Guide to International Motor Racing – Peter Higham – Guinness Publishing

The Story of Lotus 1961-1971: Growth of a Legend – Doug Nye – Motor Racing Publications

The Works Big Healeys – Peter Browning – Haynes

Journals

Autosport (With special thanks for the use of Paul's October 1967 article.)

Competition News

Motor Racing and Sportscar

Motor Sport

Motoring News

Road & Track

Small Car

Sports Car World (June/July 1986 – Barry Green)

Videos

The Gulf/Wyer GT40s & 917s in Action – Terrific Stuff Videos